Empowered

for Life

Living Day by Day in the Anointing

Sandi Lange
703-754-8696

by

Dr. Tim Bagwell

McDougal Publishing is a ministry of The McDougal Foundation, Inc., a Maryland nonprofit corporation dedicated to spreading the Gospel of the Lord Jesus Christ to as many people as possible in the shortest time possible.

Published by:

McDougal Publishing
P.O. Box 3595
Hagerstown, MD   21742-3595

ISBN 1-58158-042-8

Printed in the United States of America
For Worldwide Distribution

And the LORD *was with Joseph, and he was a prosperous man.*

Genesis 39:2

OTHER BOOKS BY TIM BAGWELL

Possessing Your Prophetic Promise
When I See the Blood
Empowered for the Call

CONTENTS

INTRODUCTION

Far too often we have thought of an anointed person only as someone who prophesies, lays hands on the sick and manifests the gifts of the Holy Spirit. I certainly would not want to detract from the importance of these very valuable ministries, but as we move forward in the twenty-first century, we need men and women who are anointed to be successful spouses and parents, and successful business and professional leaders. More and more the Lord is impressing on me the importance of Christians being anointed for daily living — *Empowered for Life.*

The gifts are wonderful, but we need to know how to cement and maintain important interpersonal relationships. Laying hands on the sick is wonderful, but we need to have supernatural power to run our businesses successfully and to carry on our professional lives with dignity and honesty. As I have contemplated this need in recent years, the life of Joseph has regularly come to mind as the perfect prototype for us to emulate, and I have found myself preaching and teaching from his experience often.

In the past, we have concentrated on Bible characters who performed great miracles, healed the sick

or had great signs following their ministries. Yet we have no record of Joseph ever having ministered to the sick or permormed great miracles. What we do know about him is that he had a gift of prophetic revelation so powerful that it moved the hearts of kings and a gift of administration so unique that it brought him to the forefront of power and accomplishment wherever he happened to be.

I am convinced that Joseph's prophetic and visionary giftings and his unique administrative talents were just part of an anointing he began to receive very early in life. This anointing resulted in a godly lifestyle that laid firm spiritual foundations in Joseph's life and later allowed him to avoid many of the traps that often cause men and women to fall and miss God's best for their lives.

For instance, when Joseph received a great prophetic promise at a very early age, he did not allow that revelation to affect his humility before God. When he knew that his brothers and even his parents would someday bow before him and that he would become a ruler over them and many others, he refused to allow the temptation to pride to hinder his relationship with God. When he was despised by his brothers, misunderstood by his father, sold into slavery, lied against and imprisoned because he would not sin with an influential Egyptian woman, and then betrayed by the king's servant, whom he had befriended and assisted, still he re-

fused to let go of his relationship with God. Joseph had realized, very early in life, that the touch of God upon everything he did was worth more than anything else, and he purposed to protect it at all costs. This enabled him to live an anointed lifestyle and to impact everyone around him.

Wherever he was and whatever he was doing at the time, Joseph lived an anointed life. Whether he was in the prison or in the palace, he maintained the attributes of one who was guided and empowered by the Spirit in all things. When the day came that he was called for by the pharaoh, he did not have to beg for time to spiritually prepare himself. Although he had been wronged in many ways by many different people, he refused to allow self-pity to smother his anointing. And when the call did come, he was ready to fulfill his destiny.

It is for these reasons that there is no greater biblical example of the anointed lifestyle God intends for His children today than that of Joseph. His entire life — the good days as well as the seemingly bad ones — was lived as a testimony to God's power. This is why I used Joseph as the grand example in my book *Empowered for the Call.* But so much more needs to be said of Joseph's life, and there is so much more that we can learn from him that I felt compelled to write this second volume, detailing more specifically this anointing for everyday life.

I am convinced that the anointing should be in

each of us, as it was in Joseph, an ever-present in-dwelling of the Spirit of God, whatever our circumstances in life. We may not feel that anointing twenty-four hours a day, but it is there nevertheless. When this is the case, it quickly becomes evident to everyone else around us. Anointed people make a mark on their world.

In Joseph, we can see at work the basic principles of faith in God and of the anointing of His Spirit and what it will do for each of us. Joseph, by his unique example, teaches us how to come into a life of God-given authority and thus teaches us how to become *Empowered for Life.*

Tim Bagwell
Denver, Colorado

Chapter 1

Empowered With Character

Joseph, being seventeen years old, was feeding the flock with his brethren; and the lad was with the sons of Bilhah, and with the sons of Zilpah, his father's wives: and Joseph brought unto his father their evil report. Genesis 37:2

Prior to Genesis 37, all that the Bible recorded of Joseph was that he was the son of Rachel, nothing more. The very first account we have in the Bible of Joseph's life demonstrates the touch of God that was upon him. He was only seventeen, but when he saw that something evil was being committed by his brothers, it repelled him. He was turned off by sin. He abhorred it. His immediate reaction was to tell his father what was being done so that it could be corrected. He simply could not tolerate wrongdoing.

This was amazing. As a general rule, teenagers are not known for their staunchness of character.

They are not renowned haters of evil. Teenagers are curious about sin and tend to experiment with anything and everything they can. They also tend to cover for each other, not to report evildoing to their parents. This may be, in part, due to the tendency of teenagers to rebel against authority. They usually side with the offenders and not with the authority figure. But Joseph was different.

It is easy to see why Jacob loved Joseph so much. This act of purity and heroism was not the first nor the last. Joseph was an obedient and respectful son, and this fact was evident in everything he did.

Jacob soon became aware that God had His hand on Joseph in a special way. Just as Abraham had become aware that everything God had promised him would come through Isaac, Jacob became aware very early in Joseph's life that God's promises to him (Jacob) would come through this special son.

Jacob had twelve sons, but this one was somehow different from the others, and Jacob soon became convinced that the things that God had spoken to him to do in the earth would not come about through Reuben or Gad or one of the other brothers. The others had not proven to be men of character. They were not known to be full of integrity. They had inherited their father's deceptiveness, the deceptiveness of Jacob, the supplanter, while Joseph had taken hold of the spirituality of Israel, prince with God.

Jacob had been a lying, deceiving and disrespect-

ful young man before his encounter with God at Bethel. In those days, he would go to any length to get what he wanted in life, and his sons had inherited that deceitful nature. Joseph, however, was like the born-again Jacob, the man with the new name and the new character — Israel, the man of vision, the man of godliness, the man of anointing.

For the majority of Jacob's sons, the end justified the means. They had no qualms about doing whatever it took to get ahead in life. They were out to tame the world, and they would use any means to accomplish their goals. They should have known better, for they were older than Joseph, but being older does not necessarily make a person better.

Joseph's brothers may have simply dismissed him and paid him little attention during his childhood, but when he became a teenager and refused to go along with their errant conduct, he suddenly became a thorn in their sides. He was acting like a prince, like a man of purpose, like a man with a mission, like a man with a holy calling upon his life, and the other brothers hated him for that.

Jacob, the deceiver, the supplanter, was well represented by his older sons, but the man had changed. He had been touched by God and had been turned into Israel, a prince who had power with God, and Joseph was emulating this new lifestyle. This delighted Jacob. Somewhere in Joseph's young life, the spirit of Israel had been imparted to him.

As Timothy received faith from Eunice and Lois, the reborn Jacob/Israel had, in some supernatural way, planted a seed of greatness into Joseph's spirit. How important it is, as godly parents and grandparents, to transfer the nature of God to our offspring!

Some may consider that Joseph was little more than a talebearer, a "tattletale," in our modern terminology, but that is not at all what the Bible describes. Joseph was not just informing on his brothers, trying to "get" them or trying to curry favor with his father. He was a young man of purpose, and he was indignant about evil. He couldn't stand it.

The Bible speaks of another man in similar terms:

> *There was a man in the land of Uz, whose name was Job; and that man was perfect and upright, and one that feared God, and eschewed evil.*
>
> Job 1:1

Job, like Joseph, prospered:

> *And there were born unto him seven sons and three daughters. His substance also was seven thousand sheep, and three thousand camels, and five hundred yoke of oxen, and five hundred she asses, and a very great household; so that this man was the greatest of all the men of the east.*
>
> Job 1:2-3

Job loved God and hated evil. When the anointing of God is upon peoples' lives, their characters become so strong that they simply cannot sit back and be silent when they see wrong things being done. They can no longer let things slip by, even though others might. Others may not seem to be bothered by the wrong that is being committed, but anointed people cannot ignore it. There are places they cannot stand to be in and situations they cannot tolerate.

Joseph also spoke out because he loved his father and was concerned about his father's welfare. His great love would not permit him to remain silent about the "shenanigans" he had witnessed in the field. He had to speak. He could not do otherwise.

As we can see, Joseph was not like some who are anointed only in the pulpit, anointed only on Sunday or anointed only in a place reserved for worship. Some people are anointed only when they put on choir robes and begin to perform. Some are anointed only when they stand on a public street corner to witness. Some are anointed only when they are called on to teach in the Sunday school. Some are anointed only during prayer meetings. But Joseph was anointed out in the field; he was anointed in the house; he was anointed in the marketplace; he was anointed of God wherever he happened to be at a given moment. He had chosen to live an anointed lifestyle.

In the years to come, the brothers of Joseph would prove to be immoral as well as dishonest. No wonder they could not stand to have their younger brother around! He could not countenance their lifestyle.

We can understand some of what Joseph faced as he took his stand for right very early in life, for in the prevailing climate of our world today it is also sometimes dangerous to be a person of character. It is unpopular and considered to be "politically incorrect" to take a stand for what is right. Joseph may have understood, even as a youngster, the price he would pay socially, within the confines of his family and community, for doing the right thing. Still, he could not do otherwise.

Anyone can follow the crowd, but when Joseph determined that he would walk the straight and narrow way, that quickly set him apart from the others. This might have been cause for concern. After all, his brothers were older and bigger and meaner (as he would soon learn). That might have been enough to intimidate others into "going along to get along." Most people, when confronted with this situation, would have decided, at the very least, not to do anything to rock the boat. Joseph didn't take this attitude, because he couldn't. He blurted out the truth, because he could not keep silent.

The evil being done by Joseph's brothers apparently concerned money, and money has become such

an idol in our time that most people will do almost anything to get it. Far too many people will bend any knee and compromise any belief for financial gain. Sadly, this is true even among Christians.

For instance, in most Christian circles, it is now considered to be totally acceptable and even "understandable" if someone misses church to make money, if someone misses prayer to make money, and even if someone makes a compromise to make money. For many, money has become an end that justifies every means. Those who have this attitude, therefore, become little more than servants to the almighty dollar. What a sad state of affairs!

God didn't call us to be bound by the things of this world; He called us to be free. He didn't call us to let money rule over our lives; He called us to have dominion in all things.

Satan has worked hard to erode character in the hearts of modern men. I have nothing against attorneys, but our society has become so litigious that the truth matters little to most people. The most important thing seems to be: get all you can get — no matter who you hurt and no matter how much you have to stretch the truth to get it. We have become so greedy that any way at all that we can make a buck seems legitimate to most people. "After all, we have to feed our families."

When any person decides to walk in integrity,

there is a price to be paid, and the reason for this is that he or she is suddenly going against the general flow of things. The great majority of men and women everywhere act underhandedly, undercut one another, knock each other down to gain an advantage, and stretch the truth a little here and a little there for personal gain.

This is why we are so tired of politicians. It appears that most of them never intend to do what they promise during their campaigns, and many don't even believe in what they are talking about so eloquently. They are just responding to the polls, just saying whatever they think has to be said to get elected. They want our votes, and for many, that is the extent of their interest in us. They have their own agendas, ones that have nothing to do with what is good for the nation and the people.

This flood of insincerity and ungodliness is so pervasive that the tendency is to just go along with it. After all, it is hard to swim against the tide. God, however, has made a sacred promise to those who are *"upright in heart"*:

> *My defence is of God, which saveth the upright in heart.* Psalm 7:10

God is our Defender; He will save us. He is our *"buckler,"* or shield:

He layeth up sound wisdom for the righteous:
he is a buckler to them that walk uprightly.

Proverbs 2:7

When we make a conscious decision to go against the tide, although we see that everyone around us is playing the game of life, it can be a very lonely feeling. It may become all the more so if we notice that others, who are ruled by the money god, seem to be getting ahead in life, while we, guided by scriptural principles and godly values, can't seem to see where our values are getting us in life. We must cling to the assurance that God has established a shield of protection for us. He is our Defense. He is our Salvation. He has promised:

Many sorrows shall be to the wicked: but he that
trusteth in the LORD, mercy shall compass him
about. Be glad in the LORD, and rejoice, ye right-
eous: and shout for joy, all ye that are upright
in heart. Psalm 32:10-11

Mercy will encompass you. Praise God!
The Psalmist declared further:

Mark the perfect man, and behold the upright:
for the end of that man is peace. Psalm 37:37

Mark him. Identify him. Set him apart. Know who he is. Find out what is going on in his life. His lifestyle is worthy of emulation. Find out who God is blessing and get near that person, for he or she is destined for greatness.

It does not work the other way around. People of integrity don't feel at home among liars and thieves. It's one thing to minister to such people, but it is quite another thing to keep company with them. We cannot afford to do it, much less go along with their habits of life or adopt them as our own.

We must not be intimidated into thinking that we are somehow missing something, that we will ultimately lose, that we will somehow be diminished if we insist on living a godly lifestyle. Uprightness brings defense. Uprightness brings a shield. Uprightness brings mercy. Uprightness brings peace. We are on the winning side. We have *"light"* in the midst of *"the darkness"* of this world:

> *Unto the upright there ariseth light in the darkness: he is gracious, and full of compassion, and righteous.* Psalm 112:4

What a wonderful promise! If we make a conscious decision to walk in uprightness before God, we are promised light in darkness. What more could we ask for?

Darkness may try to swallow us up. We may lose some money when we decide to live upright lives. We may lose some contracts. We may lose some friends, but what we gain is so much more valuable that the balance sheet is decidedly in our favor.

When we come to Christ, we are sometimes led to give back money that didn't rightfully belong to us in the first place. This doesn't hurt much, as long as it involves small amounts. But God wants to test us on every level, and He may require that we pay back larger amounts — until it begins to hurt, and hurt a lot.

Whether the amount is large or small, the act of restitution is important. The embezzler of $100,000 did not begin on that grand scale. He first stole a single dollar. That made it easier for him to steal ten dollars. Then it was a hundred dollars, and then a thousand dollars, before the larger temptation came to him.

When we allow the Spirit of God to affect even the smallest areas of our lives, we will find no peace with taking even the first dollar. God's anointing will keep us from falling prey to the little foxes that spoil the vines and that invariably lead us deeper into sin.

Uprightness brings with it many practical benefits. When God finds uprightness in an individual, He sends illumination and revelation into that life, showing that person how to deal with the practical, everyday situations of life:

Light is sown for the righteous, and gladness for the upright in heart.   Psalm 97:11

Satan has painted us a false picture. We think of the upright as being sad individuals who have no friends because they are so weird that nobody can stand them. But God says just the opposite. The upright are destined to walk in *"gladness."* They are destined to be exalted by God and, eventually, to be honored by men as well.

If you are among the upright, you have a shield, you have a defense, you have mercy, you have light in the midst of darkness, you have salvation, you have peace. You are so blessed that you are to be envied. You will *"walk surely"*:

He that walketh uprightly walketh surely: but he that perverteth his ways shall be known.
                                                  Proverbs 10:9

This word *"surely"* means "confidently." Most people are quite confused and wish that they had some direction in life. Those who have godly character and walk uprightly are no longer confused. They have confidence. Why? Because they have a shield, they have a defense, they have mercy, they have light in the midst of darkness, they have salvation, and they have peace. What could be more wonderful?

If you are among the upright, you should be feel-

ing pretty good about yourself and your future. You can have the walk of a champion.

Being humble doesn't mean you have to walk bent over and depressed and to look walked over, kicked and thrown aside. Humility is being God-dependent, and when we are God-dependent, He becomes our defense, our mercy, our light in the midst of darkness, our salvation and our peace.

I have every right to be confident. I know that I will *"flourish"*:

> *The house of the wicked shall be overthrown: but the tabernacle of the upright shall flourish.*
>
> Proverbs 14:11

Oh, I like that! If you want to flourish, keep the anointing of God working in your life. Let that anointing form the very character of God in you, and stop worrying about what will happen if you go against the current of popular opinion.

Stop worrying so much about peer pressure and start responding to Holy Ghost pressure. Let God talk louder in your ear than He ever has before, so that His voice drowns out all those other voices vying for your attention. Let God convict you of anything in your life that is not pleasing to Him, anything that is not Christlike, and let Him make you a prince so that all can see.

I believe that on his long walk back from the field that day, Joseph was evaluating his position. "If I

tell my father what I saw," he must have reasoned, "I know exactly what will happen." He understood Reuben and Levi and Simeon and Gad and Naphtali and the others, and he knew what they were capable of. He was not acting blindly. What he said to his father was not a slip of the tongue. He did not blurt it out in a moment of weakness. Joseph was fully aware of the consequences of his actions. Still, something inside of him would not allow him to remain quiet. He could not ignore these unrighteous acts — whatever the consequences.

The truth is that it never occurred to Joseph not to tell what he had seen. His brothers may have suggested it, but it could never have originated within the heart of Joseph. He was a man of upright character.

Joseph was also wise enough to know that there was little he could do personally, as a teenager, to deal with the evil he had witnessed. He would inform his father of the situation, and then it was up to his father to do something about it. Joseph would do what he could do, and he would leave the rest in his father's hands.

We know nothing else about the situation involving Joseph and his brothers' evil actions, but this is enough. It shows us that Joseph had anointed beginnings and reveals to us the foundations of his anointed lifestyle. He was empowered with character in order to be *Empowered for Life.*

I believe that the first step in an anointed, empowered lifestyle is the development of character, or integrity. In ministry, business, family ... in all the areas that impact our day-to-day lives, character is essential to long-term success. Without it, you may succeed partially, but only with it will you succeed completely.

CHAPTER 2

EMPOWERED WITH A HERITAGE

Now Israel loved Joseph more than all his children, because he was the son of his old age: and he made him a coat of many colours. And when his brethren saw that their father loved him more than all his brethren, they hated him, and could not speak peaceably unto him. Genesis 37:3-4

The coat Jacob gave to his most beloved son was not just a fine gift. It had great significance. In ancient times, men of power, usually men of royalty, used such gifts to signify their choice of an heir. Jacob was a powerful prince who knew that one day he would pass from the scene. By giving Joseph the coat of many colors, he was signifying to everyone that he had made his choice about who would succeed him as head of the family and, therefore, head of the nation. In reality, however, it was not Jacob who made this choice, but God. God's favor was visibly upon Joseph, and Jacob was only respond-

ing to what everyone who knew the lad could already see.

Jacob's other sons refused to acknowledge what
was apparent to all, for they were jealous of Joseph's
anointing. But Jacob understood destiny. God had
raised him up to be a prince with divine power, and
when he, in turn, looked at Joseph, he saw in him the
qualities of character and integrity that he wanted in
an heir. He made his choice based on the visible evidence of the blessing of God on the life of his son.

When Jacob gave Joseph the symbolic coat, you
can be sure that everyone understood its significance. Every time Joseph walked by, people would
not say, "Oh, there goes that rebellious teenager
again." They would say, "Oh, there goes the prince,
the heir." The giving of the coat of many colors was
a prophetic act on Jacob's part. It declared to everyone that Joseph would be a man of authority.

No wonder Joseph's brothers hated him! They
were not jealous that he had a better coat then they
did. They all had good coats. They were all blessed.
They were jealous because he would inherit the leadership of the family and of the nation in the future.
They had not shown themselves worthy of it, and
they hated him because he had been favored.

In reality, the brothers probably could not understand why their father was favoring a younger son.
It is often the case that family members cannot accept the authority of one who has been favored by

God. If these family members are not spiritually sensitive, they may even begin to despise their sibling who has been favored. This was the case with Joseph.

We always expect people to get excited for us when we are blessed; but not only do they not get excited, they resent our favor with God. Rather than embrace the anointing and rejoice with us, they draw back. It frightens them when someone chooses not to be like them. They often don't understand the way God works to raise up men and women of destiny.

We are only a few verses into the story of Joseph, and already we know that he was a man of character, that he was favored of God and man, and that authority was given to him very early in life. How amazing!

The anointing of God upon our lives changes everything about us. This is far more than a passing feeling. God desires for the anointing to become a lifestyle for His people. It is not just for healing the sick and casting out devils. It is not just for the moments when we are in church. It is for our daily lives — the whole of our daily lives.

The anointing of God is for the advancement of our careers. It is for the running of our households. It is for the enrichment of our marriages. It is for every dimension of our lives. If we fail to understand this, we may be living in ten percent or less of what God has for us.

Jacob was a wise man and must have known that giving Joseph such a special coat would cause problems within the family. Still, he could not help himself. He had to perform the prophetic act for all to see, signifying that Joseph would be a man of great authority.

The coat was a visible sign of the inheritance that would belong to Joseph, and it was this that enraged his brothers. They didn't hate Joseph because he had a "cool" coat. They hated him because the coat signified his father's decision to place family authority one day in his hands.

Because of Joseph's godly character, he found favor with those around him — in this case, with his father. The authority that his special coat symbolized was not given to him on a whim. It was not because he was the son of the favorite wife, as many imagine. It was the result of his godly character and the touch of God upon his life.

Some time would pass before Joseph's gifts became evident to everyone, but they were resident in him early in his life because he had chosen to go God's way, and Jacob somehow recognized this fact. The coat said, "I favor you above all my other sons," but there was a reason for that. Joseph was worthy of special recognition because of his God-given character.

The coat signified Joseph's right to lead the family when his father was gone. That was a big

responsibility for a young boy, but Joseph was being divinely prepared for great responsibility. How this was revealed to Jacob we can only imagine, but he knew it.

Did the coat say to the other brothers that Jacob loved Joseph more than he loved his older brothers? Maybe it did, but if it was true, it was because of the path Joseph had chosen, not for any other reason. The coat said to the brothers: Joseph will one day be in charge. God was about to reveal this to Joseph himself.

It never occurred to Joseph not to wear the coat his father had honored him with. That it might offend his brothers and that he would be better off not having it on never crossed his mind. He was empowered with a heritage so that he could be *Empowered for Life.*

I believe that a key understanding in living an anointed, empowered lifestyle is to embrace the knowledge that you have a God-given future, with an inheritance. To know that you are an heir of God is to know that there is preordained blessing waiting for you. To be a possessing heir, you must mature; according to Galatians 4:1, *"The heir, as long as he is a child, differeth nothing from a servant, though he be lord of all."* To have the revelation that God esteems you so highly that He has made you His heir should release confidence in you to achieve your dreams — whether they be for ministry, business or family. You have a God-given future. Wear your coat of many colors proudly.

CHAPTER 3

EMPOWERED WITH A DREAM

*And Joseph dreamed a dream, and he told it his
brethren: and they hated him yet the more.
And his brethren said to him, Shalt thou indeed
reign over us? or shalt thou indeed have dominion over us? And they hated him yet the more for
his dreams, and for his words.*

Genesis 37:5 and 8

When Joseph had a dream and told his brothers
about it, they hated him even more. Things were bad
enough between them already. They already hated
him for not participating in their sin. They already
hated him for reporting their wrongdoings to his
father. They already hated him because he was favored by his father and had been identified as the
eventual heir, but now things got decidedly worse.
Suddenly this teenager had power. Gifts were being demonstrated through his life. He was suddenly
a visionary and was foretelling the future.

Now it was a lot more than a coat. Now Joseph was making a prophetic declaration about what God had promised him. Joseph was no longer just a favorite son; he was now a dreaming prophet. In their bitterness against him, his brothers began to call him *"that dreamer."* Rather than recognize and embrace his gift, they ridiculed both him and his God-given abilities.

Because Joseph was young, he didn't have any better sense than to just tell his brothers exactly what he had seen, to describe exactly what God was showing him. He was not mature enough to know how offensive this whole matter would sound to them. All he knew was that God had revealed something to him, and in his zeal, he was telling it openly and eagerly.

This naivete about human nature can be forgiven Joseph. He was never one to pull back from the call of God upon his life, and he could not be expected to understand those who did. Light and darkness have little in common. The consequence of Joseph's naivete, however, was that his brothers hated him more every day.

Many people, when they discover that there is a price to be paid for the anointing, choose instead to shrink from it. The price seems much too high for them, and they are not willing or ready to pay it. Satan, of course, distorts the matter and tries to make us believe that we are losing something very impor-

tant by losing relationships that we have judged to be very important.

When men *are* willing to pay a price for their anointing, they are often misunderstood. Since others are not willing to pay such a price, they don't understand those who are. They misunderstand anointed people and accuse them of pride or arrogance or self-exaltation.

Because it is not intellectually acceptable or fashionable or politically correct to have God's touch on your life today, many resist it. They would rather be popular than anointed. They would rather be accepted than have an anointed lifestyle. They would rather be lauded by men than have the touch of God on their lives.

The anointing doesn't fit into man-made schedules or calendars. It doesn't fit into man's long-range plans. So carnal men reject it outright.

These are the same people who, in the day of their calamity, will travel a long distance to find an anointed person to pray for them so that their immediate needs can be supplied. They recognize and appreciate the anointing in others, but they are not willing to pay the price to have it in their own lives.

None of those to whom Joseph was compelled to tell his dreams seemed to appreciate the greatness of what God was preparing him for. He was excited, and the fact that nobody else got excited about his dreams did not keep him from reveling in their sig-

nificance. He refused to allow the hatred, the rejection and the rebuke of others to kill his dream.

The dream of Joseph related to future authority. In the dream, he saw his brothers bowing to him, submitting themselves to his authority. This thought infuriated them: *"Shalt thou indeed reign over us?"* they asked. *"Shalt thou indeed have dominion over us?"* What a horrible thought it was for them to imagine that a brother, one they already hated (and just a boy at that), would rule over them. What could be worse than serving someone you hated? And so they hated him even more.

Joseph's brothers hated him for his character, they hated him for his heritage, and they hated him *"for his dreams."* They hated him for being so spiritual, they hated him for being presumptuous enough to tell them the dreams, and they hated him for what the dreams represented.

It never occurred to Joseph not to tell the dreams, and it never occurred to him to stop dreaming just because someone didn't like his dreams or because someone did not believe in them. And then, because Joseph did the right thing with the first dream, God gave him a second dream:

> *And he dreamed yet another dream, and told it his brethren, and said, Behold, I have dreamed a dream more; and, behold, the sun and the moon and the eleven stars made obeisance to me. And*

he told it to his father, and to his brethren: and
his father rebuked him, and said unto him, What
is this dream that thou hast dreamed? Shall I
and thy mother and thy brethren indeed come to
bow down ourselves to thee to the earth? And
his brethren envied him; but his father observed
the saying.   Genesis 37:9-11

Joseph didn't just have a single dream. He became a man of dreams. His anointing was not for just a moment. It was a consistent part of his everyday life. He developed a special gift in dreams and their interpretation, a gift that would one day lift him to greatness. He could not let that gift die in its incubation period just because others failed to appreciate it. He had to nurture it and allow it to grow. He would not allow the rejection of his family to abort what God revealed.

Even Jacob didn't understand this second dream. He could not imagine that he and his wife would one day bow themselves before their son, as the dream had indicated. That made no sense whatsoever to Jacob, for parents simply did not bow to children in the cultural climate in which he lived. Jacob could not imagine such a thing, and so he rebuked Joseph for thinking it.

Many of the things that God declares to us in the Spirit don't make sense to us at the time. We have no way of knowing the end from the beginning, like

God does. And if our dreams and visions and prophecies don't make sense to us, how can we expect others to understand them? The revelations given to us usually don't make sense to the people who speak them to us, and they don't make sense to those who hear what is spoken. It doesn't seem to "add up." Nothing in our present thinking has prepared us for what God is saying, so we find it difficult to comprehend.

What God says sometimes does not make sense in the light of tradition or history or experience. He does unique things that may be difficult to fathom for those who don't know the circumstances that will prevail at some future time. We must stop trying to fit God into our little box. He does not work in the realm of the ordinary, where we can understand things, but in the realm of the extraordinary, where we often cannot.

In his naivete, Joseph could not understand at the time how offensive his dream must have seemed to his parents. He knew only what he was being told and was just simple enough to declare it — whether it made sense or not. Even Jacob stumbled at this word.

Telling this dream did not make Joseph's life any easier. It caused his brothers to hate him all the more. Now they also "envied him."

Jacob had mixed feelings about the dream. He was not sure how he should feel. He was offended

by what Joseph was saying, but he also recognized the anointing upon the lad's life. With the passage of time, he came to the conclusion that there must be a good reason for Joseph's dreams. He *"observed the saying."* In other words, he decided to keep an open heart and to watch to see what would happen next. He began pondering this matter in his spirit. He didn't understand it yet, but he knew there must be something to it.

When Joseph first told his father about the dream, Jacob rebuked his son, but after taking time to think about it, he was not ready to reject the message of the dream. As much as tradition demanded that Joseph be rebuked, something about what was said caused Jacob to have reservations.

The dreams of Joseph did sound rather silly. In the first dream, all the brothers were working in the field together, binding bundles of grain together. The bundle of grain that Joseph was working with suddenly came to life and stood erect. Then the bundles of the other brothers also came to life, and they all bowed in respect to Joseph's bundle. What a simple dream! If the other brothers didn't believe in Joseph's ultimate destiny, why then did they get upset about something so simple? They could have dismissed it as meaningless — if they were sure that it was meaningless.

In the second dream, Joseph saw the sun, the moon and eleven stars, and they all bowed in re-

spect to him. That sounds pretty silly, too, doesn't it? What was it then that made his brothers (and even his father, in this case) so upset? We must conclude that there were many other signs pointing to the greatness of Joseph's future. The hand of God was heavily upon his life. Surely his brothers and parents sensed what was happening with him.

The two dreams, although they may have sounded silly to someone who knew nothing about Joseph, had profound prophetic significance and unveiled Joseph's destiny. The test of the dreams and what they foretold would await a future time. But for now, Joseph was empowered with a dream in order to be *Empowered for Life.*

I believe that to live without a God-given dream is mere existence, and attaining an anointed, empowered lifestyle cannot happen without such a dream. God has never stopped speaking to His people. The problem is that we have become so busy, we seemingly do not have time to hear. He will show you the path that you will walk, the company you will build, the career you will flourish in, the godly home and marriage you are to nurture or the ministry you are to lead.

God is not about blindness; He is about vision. He will give you big dreams. I pray that you will have the faith to loose them into reality.

Chapter 4

Empowered to Serve

And his brethren went to feed their father's flock in Shechem. And Israel said unto Joseph, Do not thy brethren feed the flock in Shechem? come, and I will send thee unto them. And he said to him, Here am I. And he said to him, Go, I pray thee, see whether it be well with thy brethren, and well with the flocks; and bring me word again. So he sent him out of the vale of Hebron, and he came to Shechem.

And Joseph went after his brethren, and found them in Dothan. Genesis 37:12-14 and 17

Despite the fact that he already knew that he was destined to rule and that his brothers would one day bow to him, Joseph maintained a servant's heart. When his father called him and asked him to go check on his brothers and bring him word, Joseph did not find some convenient excuse to absolve him of his responsibility. He obeyed his fa-

ther. If he was to become a great man in God's eyes, he would have to maintain a heart like that of Jesus, the Servant.

Why should Joseph serve men who hated him? They had expressed contempt for him at every step. They hated what they considered to be his pompous attitude, hated his closeness to his father, hated his coat, hated his dreaming, yet he was called upon to serve them. This could not be easy, but it was required.

I find that there are basically three types of people in the church: opportunists, parasites and servants. An opportunist finds a good time to climb aboard the bandwagon. He sees when someone is destined for the top, and he conveniently hitches his wagon to the rising star and rides along. He has little concern about how he may contribute to the process. He's concerned about benefiting personally from the success someone else paid a price for.

Parasites get all they can get from a situation without putting anything back into it. They say, "I need this... I want this ... I have to have this ...," and they are often the first ones in the prayer line. But if you ask them to help you with something, they suddenly realize that it's very late and they need to be on their way. They find it very difficult to take the time to help others. They are constantly preoccupied with self.

The church needs prayer warriors, teachers, nursery workers, greeters, weed pullers, carpet sweepers and wall painters, and these positions are never filled by either opportunists or parasites. Great churches are built and maintained by servants, by men and women who have such a love for the House of God that whatever the need happens to be, whatever the demand is at a given moment, you can always count on them.

These are the Elishas of our age, the elder brothers who are in the field doing the work faithfully when the prodigal son comes back from his wandering. These are the Jabezes of our time, for Jabez was *"more honourable than his brethren"* (1 Chronicles 4:9). These are men and women deemed worthy by God of a double-portion anointing.

When we decide to be God's men or God's women, at times our personal lives are violated and we cannot always do what we want to do. The phone rings when we don't want it to ring. Somebody counts on us when we don't want to be counted on. Somebody depends on us when we don't feel like having any dependents. Somebody looks up to us when we don't feel much like being a mentor. Just when we want to relax a little, get away from it all and have some time alone, someone needs our help.

This is where many people draw the line. They want God's anointing upon their lives, and they

want to walk in authority, but they simply cannot handle the price that is involved. The life of service makes far too many demands on them.

We all want enlargement, but the process of enlarging us may not immediately bring us the personal benefits we anticipate. We may be able to help a lot more people and, at the same time, not seem to see our own situations significantly improved. Sometimes the only additions we seem to see God making to our lives are more responsibilities, more problems to deal with and more immature people to handle, and there seem to be few practical benefits.

When we ask God to let rivers of living water flow from our innermost beings, we must be ready to pay the price that entails. If we have a river inside of us, we have a responsibility to pour out its life-giving waters to those around us. If we want a river just to look at or just to brag about or just to ponder, we can forget God's river. This river flows for a purpose. It is for the healing of the nations, for the healing of imperfect people.

If we want God's authority and favor just to give us a respected place in the community, we need to re-evaluate our motives. God's authority in our lives requires that we become examples to those who will come under its influence. It requires a much deeper level of consecration on our part, and this is not for the average Christian.

Jesus said:

> *For unto whomsoever much is given, of him shall*
> *be much required: and to whom men have com-*
> *mitted much, of him they will ask the more.*
>
> Luke 12:48

Those who serve must give themselves for others, much as Christ gave Himself for the Church.
This requires bearing the burdens of others, taking
upon ourselves the responsibility for the spiritual
welfare of others. Service is a serious business for
serious believers.

Paul was willing to become an example to others. He declared to his followers:

> *Be ye followers of me, even as I also am of Christ.*
>
> 1 Corinthians 11:1

We are often quick to feel the pressure of having
other people counting on us, of having others looking to us for advice and direction in their lives, of
having others dependent upon us in different ways.
But when we are empowered to serve, God will
grant us the grace to carry these responsibilities,
even if the task is unpleasant or uncomfortable.

There is a price to pay for a higher place with God.
Although this is not a popular message, it is a necessary one for our time.

Whether God gives us responsibility over one or a hundred, a thousand or ten thousand, we must recognize the seriousness of His confidence in us and respond accordingly. If it means being misunderstood by others, even by many others, that is just part of the price that must be paid.

Joseph was destined for greatness, but he was not above running an errand for his father. He was not so great that he couldn't take time to check on his brothers. With his anointing came authority, and he would indeed one day rule over them all, but he understood how to develop his authority correctly. He had proper motives, and those motives led him to do the right thing — even for those who despised him.

Some people who come to church are weak and broken and hurting, and they need healing and restoration. But far too many have been in the church for long periods and have never started giving back. It's not wrong to be in the hospital, but you can't stay in the recovery room forever. There is a time to move out of rehabilitation and to begin to make a contribution, to do something useful. It is time to put yourself at the Father's disposal and ask Him, "What can I do? What can I do for my community? What can I do for my school? What can I do for the House of God? What can I do to give back a portion of what You have given me?"

Just because his brothers had a limited vision,

and just because they could not yet understand him, these were not reasons enough for Joseph to refuse to come to their aid when he was needed. When his father called, *"Joseph went."* He was empowered with a servant's heart in order to be *Empowered for Life.*

I believe that if you want to have an anointed, empowered lifestyle, you can never lose your servant's heart. Whether you have become the senior pastor of a church, the CEO of a great company or you have amassed great wealth or simply become what you have always dreamed of being, you can never lose your heart to serve. In God's Kingdom, what goes down will always come up. The key to always rising to the top is to never lose your heart to do whatever your Father would ask of you.

CHAPTER 5

EMPOWERED TO ENDURE

And when they saw him afar off, even before he came near unto them, they conspired against him to slay him. And they said one to another, Behold, this dreamer cometh. Come now therefore, and let us slay him, and cast him into some pit, and we will say, Some evil beast hath devoured him: and we shall see what will become of his dreams.

And Reuben heard it, and he delivered him out of their hands; and said, Let us not kill him. And Reuben said unto them, Shed no blood, but cast him into this pit that is in the wilderness, and lay no hand upon him; that he might rid him out of their hands, to deliver him to his father again.

Genesis 37:18-22

The hatred Joseph's brothers felt for him had been increasing over a long period of time. They resented everything about him and had grown to fear him, in a very real sense, for he seemed to always know

where he was going in life and what his purpose was. The fact that he did so well and that people liked him so much somehow seemed threatening to them. And those dreadful dreams! When they thought about the dreams, it caused cold chills to run up and down their spines.

Joseph was just so strange. He never seemed to worry about the normal things everyone else worried about. He never seemed to struggle to achieve something he had on his mind. Things came to him so easily. The dislike his brothers felt for him, therefore, was not just a matter of a personality clash or a difference of opinion. Somehow they felt that Joseph was probably quite dangerous, and the way things were going, if they didn't soon take things into their own hands, his terrible dreams just might come true. They had to stop him somehow!

The spirit that was at work against Joseph was the antichrist spirit that has always been at work in the world. It was the same spirit that tried to destroy Moses before he could come of age and lead the Israelites out of bondage. It was the same spirit that tried to kill Jesus very early in His life, to prevent Him from coming of age and fulfilling His destiny of redeeming the world from sin.

Satan knows that anointed people can destroy his kingdom. He knows that men and women, as vile as they might have been, can begin to change things around them when they become new creations and

get an anointing of the Spirit of God upon their lives. That's why he hates the anointing so much. He understands its impact all too well.

Satan knows how to appeal to the flesh and to the pride of the men and women around us. He knows how to stir them to jealousy and anger and even murder. He succeeded with most of Jacob's sons.

The majority of the brothers actually wanted to kill Joseph. Their hatred was that strong. They were all twelve of the same father, and there was a certain bond of brotherhood between them, but somehow Joseph didn't fit in. Brother or not, he was different. In the end, it was only Reuben's intervention that prevented the group from finishing Joseph off right then. The rest had been intent upon it, but Reuben convinced them otherwise.

Reuben may have wondered later why he had intervened on behalf of his younger brother. He was not all that fond of the lad and had, himself, entertained many thoughts against him. Why had he "gone soft" on Joseph? When the touch of God is upon our lives, men cannot harm us or prevent us from accomplishing our destinies in Him. God always intervenes in some way so that His will is accomplished. He often uses the desires of others to accomplish it. They think they are doing us harm, but God has something good in mind. It may also

seem to us that everything is going wrong, but the end result will be glorious — if we remain faithful to God.

In Joseph's case, it seems that Reuben suddenly had a pang of conscience and thought of how terrible it would be for his father to lose the son he loved most. Reuben didn't understand why his father felt the way he did about Joseph, but he respected him nevertheless and made up his mind to somehow save the lad and *"deliver him to his father again."*

A conspiracy is a serious thing, and Joseph was in a very lonely position, for he was one against many. Sometimes our circumstances seem to indicate that we are in serious trouble, but whatever our circumstances happen to be, that doesn't change God's plan. When we look to Him and not to circumstances, He is ready to make a way for us out of our present predicaments.

Maybe there is no Reuben to save us at the moment. It may, in fact, seem as if no one is paying any attention to us at all, that we are struggling alone to survive. But we can be assured that God is paying attention, and when we need Him, He will shake others awake and bring our predicaments to their attention. We must learn to relax in the arms of the Lord and know that everything will be all right.

God can confuse the thoughts of our enemies so that what they intended to do to us will come to naught. He has a higher purpose in allowing our

present circumstances, and we must trust Him that the final outcome will, indeed, be for our good.

God is not intent on putting His servants through hell on earth, as some might imagine. He has a specific plan that requires our present circumstances, and when we are delivered from them, we will apprehend our destinies.

We will look back on these experiences in the future and be glad that we trusted God and that He turned our trials into victories for His Kingdom. In the years to come, people who know us will realize that we should be dead, but we are alive, that we should be broke, but we are prospering, that we should be divorced, but our marriages are stronger than ever. And they will glorify God for the anointing of His Spirit that sets us apart from all others.

When we are wronged, even when it seems that there is a great conspiracy against us, we have nothing to fear. We don't need to find a way to rescue ourselves or to try to reason our way out of a given situation. We must learn to release things to God and let Him deal with them. He will somehow intervene on our behalf. He said:

> *Dearly beloved, avenge not yourselves, but rather give place unto wrath: for it is written, Vengeance is mine; I will repay, saith the Lord.*
>
> Romans 12:19

If men violate our rights, it is God's prerogative

to take care of it in His way. And if He doesn't choose to do it the way we want to see it done, that's still His business. Our part is to trust Him.

If Shadrach, Meshach and Abed-nego had shrunk from the fire of that Babylonian furnace, they would never have shown God's glory to the king and his people. When the fire was made seven times hotter, they didn't relent and backpedal. They were men of anointing, and men of anointing have nothing to fear — whatever the circumstances.

If we choose to accept God's call to swim against the tide and to change our world for His glory, He has promised that nothing will harm us:

> *Behold, I give unto you power to tread on serpents and scorpions, and over all the power of the enemy: and nothing shall by any means hurt you.*
> Luke 10:19

> *I will build my church; and the gates of hell shall not prevail against it. And I will give unto thee the keys of the kingdom of heaven: and whatsoever thou shalt bind on earth shall be bound in heaven: and whatsoever thou shalt loose on earth shall be loosed in heaven.*   Matthew 16:18-19

Joseph would not have been human if he hadn't wondered why all this was happening to him. He was to rule over many nations during the famine,

so Satan's opposition to his potential elevation could be expected. And if we expect to succeed in life, to change our homes and our communities, we must also expect and endure opposition.

In that moment, Joseph could have made the decision that being different was not worth all the hassle, that being separated unto God was too great a price to pay. But, of course, he didn't. He had consistently made decisions that opened His life to God's involvement, and he would continue to do so — although the benefit to him was not to appear in its fullness for many years to come.

He did not fight back against his brothers' treachery, and he could have. After all, he was no longer a child. Surely he could have defended himself in some way. It would have been very normal for him to lash out at them. But he didn't. Character always returns good for evil. Character always leaves judgment with God. Character always refuses to be cowed by wrongdoing. And since Joseph was a man empowered with character, he could stoop to none of these things.

When we refuse to get petty, when we refuse to get down in the mud and fight with people — even though they may do us wrong, steal from us and try to destroy our good names — God will give it all back to us in time — and much, much more. The life of Joseph proved this to us, for neither Reuben's plan nor the plan of the other brothers

came to fruition. God had a much greater plan for His servant. The lad must get to Egypt, and to do that he first had to endure the loneliness of the pit and the humiliation of the chains of slavery. To arrive at a place of destiny, he had to be empowered to endure what he did not understand:

> *And it came to pass, when Joseph was come unto his brethren, that they stripped Joseph out of his coat, his coat of many colours that was on him; and they took him, and cast him into a pit: and the pit was empty, there was no water in it.*
>
> Genesis 37:23-24

We can only imagine what was running through Joseph's mind as he sat in that pit. He surely must have been rehearsing all the things that led up to that moment. He must have wondered why God had permitted this to happen. In his dream, he had seen his brothers bowing to him, but they were not bowing now. They were mocking him, and they had put him in this terrible hole.

Many of us, if we were subjected to the treatment that Joseph endured, would have fallen into a deep depression and had to be taken from the pit directly to a hospital. I can't say with certainty what Joseph was thinking, but the fact that he survived the pit leads me to believe that he was rehearsing the promises of God. It was not immediately clear

how they would all come to pass, but he knew that God was faithful and that He would work it all out somehow.

Was Joseph considering the fact that things could get worse? Probably not, but they did — very quickly:

> *And they sat down to eat bread: and they lifted up their eyes and looked, and, behold, a company of Ishmaelites came from Gilead with their camels bearing spicery and balm and myrrh, going to carry it down to Egypt. And Judah said unto his brethren, What profit is it if we slay our brother, and conceal his blood? Come, and let us sell him to the Ishmaelites, and let not our hand be upon him; for he is our brother and our flesh. And his brethren were content.*
> *Then there passed by Midianites merchantmen; and they drew and lifted up Joseph out of the pit, and sold Joseph to the Ishmaelites for twenty pieces of silver: and they brought Joseph into Egypt.*
> Genesis 37:25-28

How long Joseph endured that pit we don't know. But as he sat there pondering his fate, his brothers were having a nice meal together. It didn't seem to bother them at all that their younger brother was sitting in the darkness of the pit. They felt somehow relieved. Joseph was dangerous, he was threat-

ening, he was risky, and they felt better with him restrained and out of sight. Maybe life would get back to normal now. Maybe things would come their way now that Joseph was removed from the scene. They had their thoughts, but God had His too.

God had used Reuben to save Joseph and prevent his other brothers from killing him, but Reuben's intention to return the lad to his father was not to be realized. Joseph was not to see his father again for many years. If he had known that fact, it surely would have caused him great anxiety. But what God had shown him for his future was not sadness and destruction; it was exaltation and greatness; and he had to keep focused on those promises. If we consider the race and not the prize, we quickly tire. Keeping our eyes on the prize allows us to keep running the race. It empowers us to endure.

Joseph was human, and surely he was tempted to fear. Surely he was tempted to despair. Surely he was tempted to doubt, for all men are tempted in these ways. Joseph fought the temptation to lose hope by keeping God's promises uppermost in his mind. God had a great plan for his life, and it was going to be interesting to see how God would bring it all to pass. His faith was still high, despite the terrible circumstances in which he found himself.

Now God used another of Joseph's brothers, Judah. What Judah's motivation was in saving Joseph's life is not clear. *"He is our brother and our*

flesh," he told the other brothers, hoping to convince them to go along with his plan. It may well have been another part of Judah's reasoning, however, that convinced both him and the other brothers to spare Joseph's life. There was no *"profit"* in killing Joseph, Judah reasoned. He seems to have been saying that Joseph was worth more to them alive than dead. *"Let us sell him to the Ishmaelites"* seems to have been the argument that won the votes of all the brothers.

Oh, they were elated! What a wonderful idea! They could rid themselves of Joseph, rid themselves of his character, rid themselves of his foolish dreams and rid themselves of the threat of his growing influence in the family, return things to normal, and earn a tidy *"profit"* in the process. Why hadn't they thought of that plan? It was perfect. They were all *"content"* with the decision.

Within minutes, Joseph was being pulled from the pit, but not to be returned to his father, not to have his beloved coat put back on him, and not to be restored to family and friends. Instead, he was handed over to a group of rowdy foreigners who quickly bound him and roughly pushed him in among other slaves whom they were transporting for sale in Egypt.

This was a totally new turn of events for Joseph! Who were these men, and what did they intend to do with him? It was one thing to be in the hands of

his brothers. At least he knew them. These men were strangers, an unknown quantity. Now, as the caravan made its way to Egypt, Joseph would have a lot more time to ponder his fate, time to think over his decisions in life, time to examine what had befallen him, time to either reconsider his course in life or make a fuller consecration to the call of God that was upon him.

What an interesting time that must have been! Ready or not, Joseph was being thrust into a whole new phase of his life. He had grown up rather spoiled and protected by his father, and now he would be totally on his own. There was no one to talk to, no one to pray with, no one from whom he could seek advice. He would soon learn if he could stand on his own two feet, if he could make it in the real world. Joseph had to be empowered to endure if he was to be *Empowered for Life.*

I believe that a great virtue in possessing an anointed, empowered lifestyle is that of being able to endure hardship. Hardship comes in many forms, from economic duress to relational rejection and betrayal, and even physical complications in our bodies. If we are to achieve what we are destined to do — in career, family or ministry — we will have to endure some situations that are designed to bring us revelations.

Sometimes we just have to make ourselves take another step forward and then simply keep going. If we choose to endure, we will possess what God has prepared for us.

Chapter 6

Empowered to Succeed

And Joseph was brought down to Egypt; and Potiphar, an officer of Pharaoh, captain of the guard, an Egyptian, bought him of the hands of the Ishmaelites, which had brought him down thither. And the Lord was with Joseph, and he was a prosperous man; and he was in the house of his master the Egyptian. And his master saw that the Lord was with him, and that the Lord made all that he did to prosper in his hand. And Joseph found grace in his sight, and he served him: and he made him overseer over his house, and all that he had he put into his hand.

And he left all that he had in Joseph's hand; and he knew not ought he had, save the bread which he did eat. And Joseph was a goodly person, and well favoured. Genesis 39:1-4 and 6

We can only imagine the sights and smells of the journey into Egypt with the Ishmaelite caravan. We

can only imagine how Joseph was treated, what he was given to eat and what he had to endure along the way. What is sure is that he was suddenly thrust into a new and very strange world, a world in which his role had dramatically changed, and he would have to learn a lot quickly and make some serious adjustments if he was to survive for long.

We can imagine the scenes at the Egyptian marketplace, how Joseph was displayed and examined, and how he eventually ended up in the house of an Egyptian officer, Potiphar. All of this was told by the Bible in only one sentence. He was brought down to Egypt and Potiphar bought him, the Bible shows. Whatever else he suffered in the process we are not told. This means that in the light of eternity it was not important. Joseph was empowered to endure.

As far as we know, Joseph never told the story either. He had some very important matters to concentrate on, and he couldn't afford to be caught up in self-pity. The details were unimportant. He got to Egypt, meaning he survived whatever hardships were thrust upon him, and he was purchased by an Egyptian soldier. What plan did God have now? That was the important thing, not the indignities Joseph suffered along the way.

The very next thing we know is that Joseph, miraculously, was in charge of Potiphar's affairs. Wait a minute! How did that happen? It was very unusual, to say the least. We could also use phrases

like "unheard of" and "highly unlikely to occur." An Egyptian military officer entrusted everything he had to a Hebrew slave boy. How truly amazing!

This didn't happen overnight. Although we don't know exactly how many years Joseph spent serving Potiphar, we do know that the position he was given was earned through faithful service over time. God's anointing was upon Joseph to make him excel in adverse circumstances. He was empowered with character, he was empowered with a heritage, he was empowered with a dream, he was empowered to serve, he was empowered to endure, and he was empowered to succeed.

Joseph could have complained that he wasn't called to do domestic service, but it wasn't in his spirit to complain. He was looking at the larger picture, anticipating what God would bring of all this. He did what was required of him, and he did it well, so well that soon Potiphar entrusted him with more and more.

Potiphar's trust of Joseph cannot be explained in any normal way. It was a miracle, and the Bible says of that miracle: *"His master saw that the LORD was with him, and that the LORD made all that he did to prosper in his hand."* Joseph had nothing going for him in the natural, yet he had everything going for him in the spiritual, and Potiphar saw it. Truly, promotion comes from the Lord.

Before it was over, Joseph was managing Potiphar's

house, his servants, his investments — *"all that he had."* Potiphar so trusted Joseph that he no longer kept track of what he did have. He intuitively knew that Joseph was to be trusted, so he left it all in the hands of his able and trusted servant.

Isn't it amazing that Joseph's own brothers refused to recognize his gift and, ultimately, did what they had to do to get him out of their sight, while this pagan military man embraced Joseph's anointing and put it to good use in his own house? When Potiphar saw that everything that Joseph touched was blessed, he handed more and more over to the lad.

But where did Joseph learn how to manage a household? Where did he learn how to invest money? Where did he learn how to manage personnel? He was just a slave boy. This is why Joseph's testimony has rung true throughout the generations. We cannot explain it away. Joseph was not only gifted to dream prophetic dreams, but he was also anointed to manage resources and finances. Joseph's success was a result of God's hand upon his life.

There is no way we can attribute Joseph's success in Egypt to a good education, a fine opportunity in life or the help of family and friends. Joseph had nothing going for him in the natural. Everything was against him, and still he prospered.

You couldn't keep this man down. You couldn't keep him in a pit. His brothers may have stripped

him of the coat that spoke of his favor and coming authority, but they were powerless to remove the favor and coming authority from his life. He was destined for success, and he knew it and would let nothing and no one stand in his way.

The statement here — *And the LORD was with Joseph, and he was a prosperous man* — has to be one of the most amazing statements in the entire Bible. How is it possible that Joseph was prosperous? Potiphar had bought him at some slave auction and brought him home to work in his house. And God was with him? And he was a prosperous man? How could that be?

Joseph must have wondered himself what exactly was taking place. He had been raised as the son of Jacob, a man of great riches and stature. He had been esteemed above his brothers and, because of it, was given the coveted coat of many colors as a symbol of his great future in the family. Then the very brothers he was to lead had turned on him and sold him to the Ishmaelites, and they, in turn, had sold him to Potiphar.

Joseph was being traded around like cattle. He had already been sold twice, and if he didn't do well in Potiphar's house, he would be sold again. He now had an Egyptian master over him, and he did what he was told to do. He was not free to come and go as he wished, for he was a slave. Does that sound like prosperity?

"Prosperous" in this context means that Joseph was successful. It doesn't matter what our circumstances happen to be. What is important is God's intention toward us. That changes everything.

I don't know if Joseph had any money at all. Probably not, for he had been sold into slavery. The Ismaelites would have stolen anything left on his person. He had lost his beautiful coat and was now being traded around like a used car, yet God said that He was with him and that *"he was a prosperous man."*

Joseph was not a failure, even if he didn't have a dime to his name. Success in the eyes of God is very different from success in the eyes of the world. When God rules over every detail of your life, you are guaranteed success.

If you look at the circumstances of your life, you may not agree with God that you are prosperous. So stop looking at circumstances and start seeing yourself as God sees you. If you listen to the reports of your relatives or your co-workers, you will be overwhelmed by the hopelessness of your circumstances. Look to the prophetic intention of God concerning your life, not to the hand that life seems to have dealt you.

Refuse to succumb to the negative circumstances, and cling to God's prophetic promises. Yes, you will need more resources than you have right now to accomplish all that God has promised you, but He will

provide the necessary resources in His own time. Don't let your lacks hold you back.

Joseph *"found grace in [Potiphar's] sight."* This word *"grace"* means "favor." Because he was empowered with favor, he was elevated to the position of overseer over all that Potiphar had. This took place in a relatively short time. That's what God's anointing will do for us. It gives us favor with men.

Potiphar was not a believer, by any stretch of the imagination. He did not worship Jehovah. He was also not Joseph's fellow countryman. Still, God gave His servant favor with the man, and a pagan turned everything in his house over to a Hebrew. What a miracle!

Many Christians today never know this type of anointing, this type of favor, this type of prosperity, and it is because they live such lukewarm lives. They have made a conscious decision to compromise their experience because they worry about fitting in and being accepted by others. Consequently, they miss God's very best.

If we are to attain to God's very highest for our lives, we must walk in the revelation that we are who God says we are. We must walk in the revelation that the Spirit of God is with us. In the eyes of God, we are already successful, we are already prosperous, even if the circumstances of our lives seem to be negative. At some moment and in some way, God will give us favor in the sight of our adversaries.

Potiphar was so impressed that he made Joseph the overseer of his house. This shows me that Potiphar was a perceptive man. The blessing of the Lord was upon Joseph, and it was now *"upon all that he [Potiphar] had in the house, and in the field."* God wants to place His people over companies and over industries and over new technologies, and through this, He wants to show the world His power and excellence.

When Jacob had lived for a time with his father-in-law, Laban, the household of Laban was blessed, and Laban recognized that God had done it. Now Joseph, as Jacob's heir, was carrying on the tradition of bringing God's blessing upon those around him. It didn't matter that Potiphar, as a pagan, was, perhaps, not worthy of God's blessing. He was blessed because Joseph was blessed.

When the sacred anointing oil of the Old Testament was poured upon the head of the priest and it ran down over his garments, he could not hide the fact that he was anointed. Everyone knew it. They could even smell him coming. That frankincense and the cassia and aloes were so strong, so potent, that everywhere that priest went people could smell his anointing. He couldn't hide it. And if God's anointing is on your life, you won't be able to hide it either. You can't disguise it. When you are anointed, people around you will know it.

Many born-again believers have been suffering from a persecution complex. They grew up believing that no one would receive them, that they would forever be rejected of men and they could have no success whatsoever in life. But this is contrary to the anointing. Joseph didn't believe this way at all. When one door was closed to him, he looked for another door to open. When his brothers rejected his gift, he looked for those who would recognize it.The tests and trials are for a seaon of refinement and maturing, but God's favor is for a lifetime.

God will give you favor in your personal life. He will give you favor in your business. He will give you favor in your ministry. His will is to make His favor upon your life so obvious that no one can deny it.

You will not be blessed because you are smarter than others. You will not be blessed because you try harder than others. You will be blessed because the Spirit of God is in your life. You are anointed and have the favor of God.

God was with Joseph, and that fact was evident to everyone around him. Stop worrying about the people who misunderstand you and hate you and throw you in pits and sell you out. God has a plan for your life. Rejoice in it! You are already successful and prosperous. Your life is bigger than the moment.

As Joseph was departing from his homeland, his brothers had not pressed gold coins into his hand and whispered, "Joseph, have a safe trip." They hadn't purchased for him a first-class ticket on the best airline and invited him to have a few days of vacation in Cairo. They had stripped him of his coat, spilled blood on it and lied to their father, saying that Joseph had been killed by a wild animal. Then they had thrown him into the pit and, later, sold him to a wandering band of merchants. Still, Joseph was a prosperous man. Oh, I like that! If it can happen for Joseph, it can happen for you.

If you will see God for who He is and see yourself for who He says you are, nobody can hold you back. Nobody can prevent you from achieving your goal. Nobody can keep you from greatness. You are anointed, and anointed people are destined to rise.

The Savior is with you and in you. The Healer is with you and in you. The Baptizer in the Holy Ghost is with you and in you. Jehovah Jireh, your Provider, is with you and in you. Jehovah Shalom, the Lord of Peace, is with you and in you. El Shaddai, God Almighty, has taken up residence in your life, and there is no way you can fail. You are destined for success.

He is Jesus, the Alpha and the Omega, the beginning and the end, the first and the last, the Lily of the Valley, the Bright and Morning Star, the

Blessed Rose of Sharon. And He has a plan for your life that nothing and no one can destroy.

Never mind that people are circulating negative reports about you. Never mind that they are saying that you don't have it in you to fulfill the vision. Never mind that they are saying that you'll never make it. Stop listening to what everyone else says, and start hearing what God says about you. You were not destined to be a slave; you were destined to rule. You are empowered with a dream.

Some of you have heard all your lives that you could never amount to anything because you are not as intelligent as a sibling, and you have begun to believe that lie. You have been told so many negative things by your peers that you have started to believe them. It is time to hear from God and to believe what He tells you.

Instead of saying, "I hope this works out," you need to stand in front of your mirror each morning and say to yourself, "All that I set my hand to will surely prosper because the Lord is with me, and I am empowered to succeed."

Some people fail at one thing after another, until they are sure they will always fail. It must not be so for God's people. We are destined for success, and no one can prevent it from happening.

Now, Joseph was again riding high. He had become the overseer in the house of Potiphar. All his

master's goods were under his control. He was over the entire staff, and Egyptian people respected him and moved at his command. He was empowered to succeed in order to be *Empowered for Life.*

I believe that when we live an anointed, empowered lifestyle, we will prosper and succeed. When the presence of God is on our lives, He will empower us to prosper and enhance our abilities to do all that we do with excellence. I believe God will put the spirit of Wisdom, God-given ideas and supernaturally inspired creative thinking into our lives to cause us to be the head and not the tail.

CHAPTER 7

EMPOWERED WITH HOLINESS

And it came to pass after these things, that his master's wife cast her eyes upon Joseph; and she said, Lie with me.

But he refused, and said unto his master's wife, Behold, my master wotteth not what is with me in the house, and he hath committed all that he hath to my hand; there is none greater in this house than I; neither hath he kept back any thing from me but thee, because thou art his wife: how then can I do this great wickedness, and sin against God?   Genesis 39:7-9

Things were going very well for Joseph. For the first time in many years, people around him were recognizing his unique gifts and appreciating the touch of God that was upon his life. Since coming to Egypt, he had risen meteorically from the position of simple slave to being the overseer of the estate of Potiphar. The future was looking bright, and

this helped Joseph to forget his mistreatment at the hands of his brothers and at the hands of the cruel camel drivers who had brought him to Egypt. They had not understood the plan of God, but it was becoming more clear now to those who knew him.

He had not been able to contact his parents or his brothers, but he was confident that they, too, would see God's hand on his life at some point. Surely that would become possible someday — somehow. After all, God had shown it to him in dreams.

Then something absolutely terrible happened to Joseph, something so unexpected that it took him completely by surprise. His master's wife began to cast her eyes lustfully upon him. It may seem utterly absurd to some that a woman of such high estate would consider such a risky relationship, but, believe me, it's not. The anointing makes you unique and brings out special characteristics in you that are attractive to other people. Those who are spiritual recognize this as the Spirit of God drawing them, but those who are of the world cannot identify what they are being drawn to.

Potiphar's wife couldn't help but notice that Joseph was unusually compassionate. He was understanding and caring. He was sincere and honest and meant what he said. She liked that.

Sure, Joseph was good-looking, but he was also a slave who had nothing to offer. There was more to this sudden move by the master's wife than mere

physical attraction. She desired to be identified with Joseph's spirit, and the only way she knew how to do this was through a physical relationship.

This was a tragic turn of events for Joseph. He was lonely, he was far from home and he was honored that this prominent woman would be interested in his affections. Still, he was not about to sin with her, and he must have sensed from the start that his resistance would cause problems. It could not be any other way. Still, he had no alternative.

Some of us might have thought long and hard about the wisdom of angering a prominent Egyptian woman if we had been in Joseph's situation. After all, things were going well. Why rock the boat? Why upset the master's wife?

But Joseph didn't have to think long and hard about his response. He quickly said, *"How then can I ...?"* meaning, "How could I do that?" or simply, "I can't do that." He just couldn't. His integrity would not permit him to do it. His holiness would not allow it. His godly character would not give him permission. The anointing on his life caused him to resist anything that would sidetrack him from God's plan for his future.

Joseph valued the empowerment of God on his life more than he valued some quick gratification of the flesh. He was not about to sell his inheritance for a bowl of porridge, like his Uncle Esau had done. He was not ready to compromise for personal gain.

Potiphar had been good to him, had trusted him and had placed all his possessions in his hands. Yielding to this temptation would be a sin against his master. More importantly, it would be a sin against his God.

Joseph valued his relationship with Potiphar. The man may have been a pagan, but he had a good heart, and he was able to recognize the Spirit of God when he saw it. But how much more Joseph valued his relationship with God! When he had been in that pit, during the time he had traveled with those foreigners in the caravan and could not communicate with them, and when he had first arrived at the house of Potiphar and everything had been new and strange to him, God had been his only companion. He had suffered the wrath of his brothers because of his closeness to God. How could he simply abandon that relationship now? He had the right answer. He could not.

For Joseph to sin against his master would be to sin against his God, and besides, God had not sent him to Egypt to get embroiled in its fleshpots, but to become its prime minister. Joseph had to keep himself pure and prepare for the day of his supreme service. He could not get sidetracked into fleshly pursuits.

Sometimes, because we can see the people around us and are keenly aware of their presence and know that we will be seeing them over a pe-

riod of time, it is easier for us to think of not wanting to hurt them than it is to think of not wanting to hurt God. As a result, we are slow to offend people, and quick to offend God. Still, it is many times more important not to offend God than it is not to offend one another.

Those of us who love the Lord passionately do not want to do anything to grieve His Holy Spirit or anything to quench His operation in our lives. We are careful not to do anything to cause the Holy Spirit to withdraw Himself from our presence. We have too much to lose.

Those who fail to value their relationship with God are doomed to destroy it. Why is it, then, that most people put a greater value on their relationships with the people around them than they do on their relationship with God? They are careful not to hurt a friend or co-worker. "He has been so good to me," they say. "He helped me pay my utility bills when I was out of work for a while." "She prayed with me once when I was going through a difficult time. I would never do anything to hurt her."

That is good and proper, but why can't we see how important it is not to hurt God when He has been so good to us? We somehow think that God will always understand when we turn our backs on Him, that He will always look the other way when we break His commandments and that He will hang around even when we have violated every trust He

has placed in us. What a tragedy! Joseph so valued his intimate relationship with God that he dared not do anything that would hinder or destroy it — not one thing!

When we are drawn into an intimate relationship with the Lord, His holiness is imparted to us. We become holy, not *for* Him, but *because of* Him. To be holy is to be like Him by partaking of His holiness. This is not achieved through works but through relationship. The relationship does not flow from the works, but the works flow from and follow the relationship.

When we get closer to the Lord, we no longer have the desire to do certain things that before seemed perfectly appropriate. As a pastor, I wrestle with how far I can go in guiding people toward holiness. I can establish some guidelines, but it is impossible to cause people to walk righteously if they're not willing to deepen their relationship with the Righteous One so that His righteousness shows forth from their lives.

When we know Him intimately, we never feel that we are giving up something for Him or that we are somehow missing something important in life. We know that we have the very best — in Him.

Joseph did not hesitate in his answer to Potiphar's wife because there was no other acceptable answer. He didn't toy with her. He told it like it was: "I can't do this!"

It bothers me when so many Christians talk constantly of what they have given up to serve the Lord. I would like to hear them say, "Thank God, I've been delivered from the kingdom of darkness and have found the very best life has to offer. Thank God, I've been granted the greatest privilege known to man. I'm proud to be part of His Kingdom. I'm pleased to be part of His family. I gave up nothing and gained everything in exchange." When we have our priorities straight, there is no other answer.

Joseph did the right thing because it was his nature to do it. It never crossed his mind to say yes to the woman. His was the only logical choice. He could not do otherwise.

The Spirit of God is stronger than your emotions. He can override your attitudes and feelings. Paul said:

> *For if ye live after the flesh, ye shall die: but if ye through the Spirit do mortify the deeds of the body, ye shall live.*　　　　Romans 8:13

Quit trying to overcome your flesh in your own power and start crying out to God, "God, send Your refining fire. Purge me. Burn all the dross out of my life. I cannot cleanse myself, but You can cleanse me. I cannot lay down unrighteousness in my own strength. Let Your Spirit work in me." If you will do this, you will discover that living a holy life is the

easiest thing you could ever have imagined, the easiest thing you have ever done.

Most of us consider that power comes from God and gifts come from God, but that holiness must somehow come from within each of us. This cannot be true. We have no holiness of our own. There is no holiness to be found in us. Only God is holy. He is the Originator of holiness, the Manufacturer of holiness, so we must go to the Source. He is Holiness, and the closer you get to Him, the more you live in Him and move in Him and have your being in Him, the more holy you will be — because of Him, not because of you. Being with Him, you will become conformed to His image.

Holiness, then, is not a difficult thing. When you are living close to God and you are suddenly faced with the most grievous temptation that has ever come to you, the first thing that will come to your mind is how wonderful your intimate relationship is with God, how much breaking covenant with Him would hurt, and how much you would lose if anything happened to that relationship. Then it will be easy for you to say, as Joseph did, *"I cannot commit this sin against my God."*

You become more concerned about maintaining your relationship with God than about gaining a promotion on your job, about getting more money in your bank account, and about receiving the affirmation of people. The height, breadth and depth of

your relationship with God suddenly dominates your every thought, your every move and your every word. And you become holy, not because you know all the right things to do, but because you have developed an intimate relationship with the Holy One. We are *"partakers of His holiness"*:

> *For they verily for a few days chastened us after their own pleasure; but he for our profit, that we might be partakers of his holiness.*
>
> Hebrews 12:10

Holiness is nothing more than the essence of His nature. Because He is holy, being close to Him results in our partaking of that essence of His nature. We become *"partakers of the divine nature"*:

> *Whereby are given unto us exceeding great and precious promises: that by these ye might be partakers of the divine nature, having escaped the corruption that is in the world through lust.*
>
> 2 Peter 1:4

Lust will block the flow of God in our lives, but when we become more intimate with Christ, our lives totally change for the better, without our having to struggle to make it happen. If we try to give up something on our own, we only make ourselves and everyone around us miserable. So we must stop

trying to do it in our own strength and let Him do the work in us.

If you remove many things from your life and fail to replace them with God's love, you will just have a life full of gaps. The result of that cannot be joy and fulfillment. If religion has ripped your life apart, without giving you anything to replace what you have lost, this only complicates your problem. This is why the Scriptures declare:

> *And be not drunk with wine, wherein is excess;*
> *but be filled with the Spirit.*   Ephesians 5:18

Without the Spirit to replace our habits, we cannot be successful in ridding ourselves of the perceived needs of the flesh. God doesn't just take habits from us; He gives us something so much better that we no longer have need of the things that formerly filled the gaps in our lives. If we walk away from something, we must have something else to replace it, or our situation will only grow worse. Don't just try to replace your cigarette habit with chewing gum or the patch. Replace it with God.

If you are walking away from sexual perversion, you must have something to replace it, or you will find yourself going right back for more — as so many others have done. Get full of God, and you will have no desire to go out and get drunk. Get full of God, and you will have no need of drugs or illicit

sex or any of the rest of Satan's offerings. Get full of God, and you will lose the need for the vile conversation that has become your habit. Let God take your anger; let Him take your jealousy; let Him take your perversion.

God Himself will begin to strip away the things that have done you harm. Suddenly the junk will start flying off of you. You will say, "I don't need or want that anymore. I'm free, free indeed."

Even the power of Jesus was dependent on *"the spirit of holiness"* in His life. He was:

> *... declared to be the Son of God with power, according to the spirit of holiness, by the resurrection from the dead.* Romans 1:4

All of us want greater power and greater authority, and all of us yearn for greater favor, but ultimately all of these depend on the depth of *"the spirit of holiness"* that we reach in God. Get closer to Him. Get closer to the Source, and let His holiness rub off on you. *"Put on the new man"*:

> *And be renewed in the spirit of your mind; and that ye put on the new man, which after God is created in righteousness and true holiness.* Ephesians 4:23-24

God would not have to speak of *"true holiness"* if

there was no false holiness. All too many times we try to do it on our own. God, however, is not interested in our *"filthy rags."* He alone can produce in us the *"true holiness."* Our flesh cannot produce it, and anything produced by our flesh that tries to appear like holiness is a poor imitation.

It doesn't take much discernment to know the difference between true and false holiness. Self-righteousness is so apparent that it fools very few. It is no fun, even for the person who is trying to imitate holiness. It makes a person feel that he has truly sacrificed when, in reality, he has been doing exactly what he wanted to do all along.

True holiness is a joy. When it is present, we know that we have missed nothing in life, sacrificed nothing and yet gained everything in the process.

If we are forced to give something up, by a family member, a church leader or anyone else, we have not experienced the *"true holiness,"* and we will be miserable. When we give something up out of love for Jesus, no one will ever be able to take our reward from us.

When holiness is present, lying stops, sinful anger stops, stealing stops, corrupt communication stops. We no longer give a position of influence to the devil, and we stop grieving the Holy Spirit, breaking God's heart. Instead, we start doing good things, producing good fruit, speaking good things.

Malice, bitterness and anger are gone, and in their place we have love, joy and peace, longsuffering, gentleness, meekness, temperance and faith. This is why Joseph could respond so quickly to the wife of Potiphar, why he couldn't do this thing.

When the test of character comes, the carnal mind has all the reasons why sin is not so bad:

"If no one knows about it, who could possibly be hurt? She surely won't tell anyone. She has a husband who is a noted military officer, so she has every reason to keep her mouth shut about it. And I certainly won't tell anyone. What harm could it do?

"If she and her husband had a good marriage to begin with, this wouldn't be happening.

"She started this thing. I didn't initiate it, so how could anyone blame me? She approached me. She started it all. It's her fault. Surely she recognizes that fact.

"I have to think about my future. If I don't go along with her, she might ruin me. I really have no choice in the matter."

If would have been ever so easy for Joseph to yield in this situation, and lesser people would have. Joseph's godly character, however, would not allow him to do what was easy. Even if no one else knew

what he had done, he would know, and God would know, and he had to live with himself and God. Just as he had not been able to overlook the wrongdoing of his brothers, now he could not agree to sin with Potiphar's wife — even if no one ever learned the truth about what had occurred between them in a private room that day.

The empowerment of integrity led Joseph to report to his father the wrongdoing of his brothers. Now, the empowerment of holiness led him to turn and run from Potiphar's house. He had not considered the consequences when he reported the wrong to his father, and he could not consider them now. What would happen would happen. What mattered to him was his future with God, not his future with people.

I am convinced that if Joseph had yielded to the desires of Potiphar's wife, it would have destroyed him. He would have lost his integrity, lost his purpose in life, lost his gift and lost his authority. He would never have risen higher in life and would probably never have been mentioned in the Bible. Many people who lived in his time are not found in the sacred pages, for they made no impact on their generation.

Joseph ran from sin, and I am compelled to ask, "Where are your steps taking you?" Those of us who have integrity and holiness of spirit will do

as Joseph did, and if we remain upright, God will lead us into green pastures and beside still waters. He will lead us into prosperity and into peace and joy. He will open His orchards to us and allow us to partake of all the best He has to offer in life. We will become partakers of His fruit. Those who allow Satan to lead them and refuse to run from sin wind up in a thorn patch somewhere and are sometimes unable to get out of it. Joseph took the wise course of action. It may not have seemed like the "fun" thing at the moment or the humanly prudent thing to do, but he knew it was right.

Because Joseph had rejected Potiphar's wife, because he would not do what she was suggesting, she turned on him — venomously. She lied about him to her husband and set in motion a chain of events that sent Joseph to prison. Character kept Joseph from sin, and holiness lost him his job. That's how most people would look at it, and most would then compromise and feel justified in doing so. But when you stand for what is right, although you may seem to endanger your current position with your boss or with your friend, you preserve the favor of God on your life, the favor that placed you in a given position in the first place. If God had done it for him once, Joseph was sure that God would do it for him again.

So Joseph was on his way to prison, but his

spiritual integrity was intact. He was pushed into a dank cell, but he had not compromised his principles, and He was confident that God would somehow help him.

Talk about a role model! There is none better than Joseph. He was empowered with holiness so that he could be *Empowered for Life*.

I believe that in order to maintain an anointed, empowered lifestyle, we must embrace the truth that we are called of God to be holy. Not just the preacher, but the businessman and the professional as well. Not just the husband, but also the wife and the children. Compromise is diametrically opposed to holiness, but if what we lose in the natural is more valuable to us than what we would lose in the spiritual, then compromises will come easily and quickly. But never forget that God will always remember where He is positioned on your list of priorities.

CHAPTER 8

EMPOWERED WITH FAVOR

But the LORD was with Joseph, and showed him mercy, and gave him favour in the sight of the keeper of the prison. And the keeper of the prison committed to Joseph's hand all the prisoners that were in the prison; and whatsoever they did there, he was the doer of it. The keeper of the prison looked not to any thing that was under his hand; because the LORD was with him, and that which he did, the LORD made it to prosper.

Genesis 39:21-23

The Bible gives no description of the Egyptian prison into which Joseph was now unceremoniously thrust. It tells us nothing about what liberties he was given or what he was fed or how large his cell was or whether it was too hot or too cold or just how he was treated. These circumstances would seem vitally important to us, but maybe they didn't even matter to Joseph. He was ready to live for God —

no matter what. He was ready to do the right thing — however he was treated and whether his circumstances were good or bad. All we know about this particular prison was that it held prisoners put there by the king himself. That had to be a very bad place.

Things certainly did look bad at that moment for Joseph, and the general trend of the events of his life seemed to have been downward for some time. He had experienced a momentary success in the house of Potiphar, but his life was not going all that well overall. Rebuked, hated, rejected, betrayed, sold into slavery, slandered, unjustly imprisoned: this series of events was certainly something that would make anyone think seriously.

Many of us, if placed in a similar situation, would become bitter. After all, what had Joseph done worthy of imprisonment? He had refused to compromise with his brothers and had refused to compromise with his master's wife, and where had it all gotten him?

What mattered to Joseph, however, was that God was still with him. We must stop gauging God's favor on our lives by the circumstances that surround us. Storms may come, but God is there in the midst of every storm. When we insist on looking at the circumstances, we tie the hands of God. He wants to favor us, but we keep saying that it can't be done "under these current circumstances." What we don't see is that the "current circumstances" are necessary

to bring us to the height of authority that God has planned for us.

We must make the decision that in whatever circumstances we find ourselves, we will say, "I am anointed, and I have favor with God." We may not have a lot of money at the moment, but that doesn't matter. We may not feel very well at the moment, but that is not the gauge. Things may not be going well in our businesses at the moment, but God is with us nevertheless. Things may not seem to be going well in our marriages or in our families, but if God is with us, it will all work out, so nothing else matters.

I know that everyone is interested in seeing the evidence of God being with us, the evidence of His favor on our lives, and it will come. For now, the Bible teaches:

Now faith is the substance of things hoped for, the evidence of things not seen.   Hebrews 11:1

We don't have it yet, but we're hoping for it. We haven't seen it yet, but we are believing God for it. Circumstances mean nothing to us. We are looking beyond circumstances — because God is with us.

If God was not with us, we might have reason to be concerned, but He is with us, so we have nothing to fear. God can give us favor under any circumstances.

To give Joseph favor in the Egyptian prison, God had to change the heart of the pagan jail keeper, but He can do that, and He does — when we allow His anointing to keep flowing in us.

Some say to me, "Pastor, you just don't understand my situation." That may be true, but I know Him who is over every situation. Some say, "You don't understand who is opposing me." That may be true, but I know Him whose Word declares:

If God be for us, who can be against us?
Romans 8:31

Four hundred years after Joseph, another man of God, Moses, would be assured of victory in Egypt, although he would have to suffer many temporary setbacks before that victory became reality:

And I will give this people favour in the sight of the Egyptians: and it shall come to pass, that, when ye go, ye shall not go empty. Exodus 3:21

The Egyptians had come to despise the Israelites and were hard taskmasters over them. There was no way they were going to be favorably disposed toward them. But when God has declared a thing, nothing that Satan can do will stop it. God told Moses that his people would have favor with the

Egyptians, and it happened — just as God had said it would.

I am sure the Egyptians wondered why they were blessing the Israelites, when they had always despised them so much. Some of the Israelites may also have wondered, but God knew what He was doing:

> *And the LORD gave the people favour in the sight of the Egyptians. Moreover the man Moses was very great in the land of Egypt, in the sight of Pharaoh's servants, and in the sight of the people.* Exodus 11:3

God not only did what He had promised; He did it exceedingly well. This same Moses had been run out of town for killing an Egyptian, and for years he had lived in humiliation on the back side of the desert. Although he had been raised in the palace as a prince and an heir of the pharaoh, he had been forced to work as a shepherd to earn his keep. Now, because of his faithfulness, God had exalted him in the eyes of all the people. This is the mighty power of our God in action!

Moses had no army. He had come down from the mountains with a stick in his hand. He couldn't even speak properly and had to have someone else be his spokesperson. But he knew the will of God and said to Pharaoh, *"Let my people go."* Although the pharaoh resisted as long as he could, and Moses had to

pass through many trials in the meantime, in the end Pharaoh was forced to obey, for God was with Moses.

David had this same touch of God's favor on his life from an early age:

> *And Saul sent to Jesse, saying, Let David, I pray thee, stand before me; for he hath found favour in my sight.*   1 Samuel 16:22

King Saul had sinned and was destined to lose his throne. He was so far from God that he was continually tormented by evil spirits. Yet even in that state, he honored the anointed of the Lord and called upon David to help him. Eventually, David took Saul's place. In the meantime, David had to run for his life and live among thieves and castaways.

Esther obtained God's favor in a difficult situation:

> *And Esther obtained favour in the sight of all them that looked upon her.*   Esther 2:15

Esther had submitted herself to an extended period of purification and anointing, for she was preparing herself to please the king. During that lengthy period of waiting, she did not become distracted or lose sight of her goal. She had been chosen by God to free her people, and she must not fail Him or them.

At the end of her time of preparation, there was a

noticeable change in Esther. She was not only well prepared; she *"obtained favour in the sight of all them that looked upon her."* Favor doesn't come without preparation, for God has to know that He can trust us to use His anointing properly.

If we stay long enough in the presence of God, the change in our lives will be notable. Everyone will see it.

This same change was noted in the young Jesus:

> *And Jesus increased in wisdom and stature, and in favour with God and man.* Luke 2:52

He had begun life as a normal-looking baby, but now something had changed. He was moving toward His destiny, toward the fulfillment of the Father's plan for His existence on earth. He was anointed, as He would proclaim in His first messages in the synagogue.

Jesus favored certain of His disciples — Peter, James and John — and, since He is no respecter of persons, many have wondered why. It was because they stayed closer to Him than some of the others. They delighted in His presence and were always eager for His teachings. He didn't choose them over others. They chose Him more than others, and therefore they were blessed.

When it came time for Moses to pass the scepter of leadership to another generation in the wilder-

ness, he chose a younger man named Joshua. Of all the men who had accompanied him during his exploits in bringing the people out of Egypt and on their way to the Promised Land, Joshua stood out. The reason was that this young man had been enthralled with the anointing he saw in Moses, and he never wanted to leave him. As a result, he became Moses' personal aide and served him in this capacity for many years. God now led Moses to favor Joshua because He saw what was in Joshua's heart.

As Elijah was preparing to pass from the scene, he also chose a younger man to succeed him. He had overheard Elisha say, *"As the LORD liveth, I will not leave thee,"* so he knew Elisha's desire for the things of God. When any of us choose to spend more time in God's presence, the result will become visible. God's touch will be upon us, and this will bring us favor with men.

Before long, Joseph was in charge of the entire prison. This is amazing, not only because he was an alien in the land, but also because he was himself a prisoner, accused by a prominent Egyptian family. Our God is mighty, and nothing hinders His plans. Just as he had been placed in charge of Potiphar's affairs, now Joseph was placed in charge of an important Egyptian prison.

This man was more than a dreamer; he believed his dreams. Those dreams were from God, and God exalted Joseph, giving him unusual gifts and abili-

ties and giving him favor with everyone around him — even in the prison. His anointing was for daily living.

Yes, Joseph was in prison, but God was with him. He was in prison, but God was anointing him. He was in prison, but God was showing him mercy. He was in prison, but God was giving him favor, this time with the keeper of the prison.

The apostles of the early Church were persecuted, and if they had concentrated on that persecution, they could have become withdrawn and inactive, fearing to anger those around them. But take a closer look at the New Testament. All of the persecution the early apostles suffered turned into a blessing, to the furtherance of the Gospel. The early apostles were not stopped even one time from doing what God had called them to do by the persecution they faced, and they always came out on top in the end.

Every town these men went into was turned upside down for God, and you don't do that without having favor with the people.

When Philip went to Samaria and preached, for instance, God turned the whole city around. That would be impossible without having divine favor.

So Joseph was in jail. So what? He was still anointed, and he still had God's favor on his life, and that's why before long he was running the whole prison. Everything was committed to Joseph's hand for safekeeping and proper management. God was

with this man, and everyone around him knew it.

None of us wants to be thrown into a pit. None of us wants to spend time in a dark dungeon somewhere. And when it happens, we often become discouraged and think that God has forgotten us and that all is lost. If we refuse to relinquish God's anointing, however, wherever we are and whatever we happen to be doing, our ultimate victory is absolutely assured. We cannot lose.

What was Joseph doing in the prison that was so outstanding? We don't know for sure. Much of it might have seemed mundane and unimportant, but God put His seal of approval on it. Everything Joseph touched turned to gold. Everything he tried worked. Everything he suggested bore fruit. What a miracle!

Joseph had absolutely no earthly security. He was in jail. What could he count on? Still, he clung to his God-given dream. One day he *would* be rich. One day he *would* be powerful. One day he *would* be influential. So should he just sit back and wait for that day? He thought not. And that's what was great about every person of faith in the Bible. They didn't wait for tomorrow to come; they started living for God today. They didn't wait for better circumstances to come along; they started living for God under the existing circumstances.

Joseph was not, at that moment, reaping a personal harvest, but he knew that it *would* come in due

time. God never fails. Everything seemed to be against Joseph at that moment, but he was prospering anyway.

We desperately need a revelation from God. No matter what seems to be coming our way, no matter what the devil seems to be throwing at us at the moment, God is on our side, and we are guaranteed ultimate victory — if we will not lose faith in the time of trial. Joseph was empowered with favor in order to be *Empowered for Life*.

I believe that when we live an anointed, empowered lifestyle, we will always have favor — first with God and then with man. The Spirit of God in you, instead of repelling men from you, will draw people to you. They will want you to be involved with them for reasons that they do not even understand. The favor of God will always have a mysterious impact on those around you. I challenge you to make the confession: I am anointed. I have favor with God.

Chapter 9

Empowered to Wait

Yet did not the chief butler remember Joseph, but forgat him. And it came to pass at the end of two full years, that Pharaoh dreamed.

Genesis 40:23-41:1

As Joseph was conducting the daily affairs of the prison, he probably had no idea how long he would be there or how — or if — his freedom would finally come. He was still *"bound,"* and life was not what he might have liked, but he must be faithful day after day and trust God with the details of his future. Now, more prisoners were placed in his care, and *"he served them."*

One of the most powerful secrets of Joseph's success was that whatever he did, he did with excellence. That's why people were always anxious to entrust him with more. He had shown consistently that he could be trusted. Trust must always be earned; it is never a gift.

Joseph was not just organizing the food service or the cleaning crews or the other prison work crews or whatever it was in its totality that had been entrusted to him; he was also slowly but surely building up a reputation as a man who understood dreams and other spiritual matters. The gift was again called upon one day when two of the king's servants each had a dream:

> *And they dreamed a dream both of them, each man his dream in one night, each man according to the interpretation of his dream, the butler and the baker of the king of Egypt, which were bound in the prison.* Genesis 40:5

When Joseph came into the cell of these men the next morning, he noticed that they were rather despondent. He took an interest in his wards and asked what the matter was. When the men told him about having had dreams, his response was immediate and positive:

> *And Joseph said unto them, Do not interpretations belong to God? tell me them, I pray you.* Genesis 40:8

This was probably news to these men, but dreams and their interpretation was nothing new for Joseph. He had been hearing from God since

his childhood, and he was confident that God would answer him now.

The butler told Joseph his dream. He had seen a vine with three branches that budded and shot forth, first blossoms and then ripe grapes. He saw Pharaoh's cup in his own hand, and he took the grapes, pressed them into the cup and gave it to Pharaoh to drink.

Without hesitation, Joseph said to the butler, "This is the interpretation of the dream: The three branches of the vine represent three days. In three days Pharaoh will pardon you and restore you to your position, and you will again serve him."

When the baker heard this, he was delighted with the good interpretation and asked Joseph to interpret his dream also. He had seen himself with three white baskets on his head. The topmost basket contained pastries of various kinds prepared for the king, and, as he watched, birds came and ate from it.

As before, without hesitation, Joseph answered the man. "The three baskets are again three days. In three days Pharaoh will call for your execution. You will be hung from a tree, and birds will come and eat your flesh."

Most of us would have kept silent rather than bring such a message to a servant of the king, but it never occurred to Joseph not to tell the interpretation exactly as God had given it to him.

Three days later, as the king was celebrating his

birthday at a feast with all his servants, he announced that he was restoring the butler to his position but that the baker would have to be hanged. And so the two dreams came to pass in the same day.

Joseph had grown considerably in power and authority. As he had walked faithfully with God through the tests and trials of his young life, greater wisdom and greater boldness had come to him, until now he had a very powerful gift. What he spoke came to pass.

After receiving such a miraculous interpretation of the butler's dream and conveying it to him, a thought suddenly came to Joseph. Maybe this would be the tool God would use to free him. If the butler would be restored in three days and would again serve the pharaoh (and he was sure it would happen), perhaps the butler could intercede with the Egyptian monarch on his behalf. This was his chance. He boldly pleaded to the butler:

> *But think on me when it shall be well with thee, and show kindness, I pray thee, unto me, and make mention of me unto Pharaoh, and bring me out of this house: for indeed I was stolen away out of the land of the Hebrews: and here also have I done nothing that they should put me into the dungeon.* Genesis 40:14-15

When he had said this, a new excitement came to Joseph's heart. Surely this matter would now be brought to the pharaoh's attention. "Thank God," I can hear him praying as he went back down the prison corridor toward the other cells, "I'm finally going to get out of this place. The time for my deliverance must be now at hand." He had blessed a notable person, and surely this would be his key to freedom.

It must have come as a terrible shock when time passed and it finally became obvious that the man who had seemed so grateful had totally forgotten his benefactor. He had quickly and easily forgotten his commitment to remember Joseph in Pharaoh's court.

For a long while after helping the butler, Joseph had, no doubt, been expecting someone to come for him at any moment. Every time he heard a door open, he probably thought it must be one of Pharaoh's royal guards to say that the Hebrew should be freed. Alas, it never happened! It seemed that all Joseph could do was wait.

I believe that it was during this time that God was revealing to Joseph that promotion does not come from man, but from the Lord. Joseph, like us, had to learn to wait for God's perfect time.

When more months went by, and nothing had changed, Joseph had no alternative but to continue to perform his appointed tasks and wait. In time,

Pharaoh would have a dream and would need an interpretation. For now, Joseph must keep his spirits high and must keep the touch of God upon his soul. Too much was at stake to become restless just because the servant had not kept his promise.

We must learn, like Joseph, to keep doing what we know to do — even when things do not seem to be going as scheduled for us. Joseph kept his heart right with God and kept allowing the Holy Spirit to move in his life. Many of us get so flustered with the ups and downs and delays of daily life that when the time comes for us to lay hold of God's blessing, we're not sure which end is up in our own lives, and we miss the strategic moments of great opportunity.

This could be expected — if we had to face life in our own strength. But we don't. We can know that delays are not always denials, and that God is preparing us for greater things to come.

Joseph's ability to deal with his own problems and always remain ready to do whatever God positioned him to do was a result of his daily submission to the will of God.

It is understandable that Joseph asked the butler to remember him when he got out. We're all human, and most of us would have done the very same thing. It's our natural tendency to try to assist God in helping us. I believe one of the greatest keys to possessing an anointed lifestyle is to learn how to wait on God. He knows the exact moment that we

need to be positioned for season-changing break-throughs. We want everything "yesterday," "ASAP," but we must trust that God possesses insight that we do not. He really does know the future.

The king's men were well-connected, and Joseph thought, quite naturally, that they should be able to help him. After all, he was a good man; he had wronged no one; and he had proven his faithfulness — in the prison and out of the prison. He had helped both of the king's servants in their time of need, so why shouldn't the butler at this moment help him in his time of need? It made perfect sense on Joseph's timetable.

But we are blessed because we get connected with God and stay connected with God. We are strength-ened because we learn to wait on God:

> *But they that wait upon the LORD shall renew their strength; they shall mount up with wings as eagles; they shall run, and not be weary; and they shall walk, and not faint.*   Isaiah 40:31

When we insist on dictating the pace at which things will be accomplished, we are setting ourselves up for disappointment. And it will surely come.

It is the touch of God in our lives that will give us favor with those around us. It is God who opens doors for us. It is God who puts us in the right place at the right time, doing the things that will release

to us local, national or even international impact. Restlessness will drive you to try to open doors for yourself. Relax! Stop trying to open doors for yourself! Stop struggling to lift yourself to the top! Living an anointed lifestyle will lift you up effortlessly.

Opportunity that doesn't come from God is dangerous to our overall health. It somehow places more on us than we are able to bear. We often pry open doors that we later wish we hadn't tried so hard to enter, because we are not ready for what we find on the other side. Often we get more than we bargained for when we force the issue. When God does it, an open door brings with it all that we need to do the job, prosper and flourish emotionally and spiritually.

Why is it that we always think we know better than God? He has promised to supply all our needs, yet we are constantly telling Him exactly what to give us and when to release it. The Lord has promised to make all that we do to prosper, but we must learn to let Him do it in His own way and time.

Why do we doubt that He knows the right moment to release opportunity and blessing to our lives? Joseph was ready to get out of prison immediately, but if he would have left prematurely, he probably would have been no more than a gifted parolee. Pharaoh still had to dream a dream, and Joseph had to wait so that he could receive the fullness of God's prophetic promise over his life.

The demonstration of God's favor on the life of Joseph would come, but it would come in God's way and in God's time. When it came, Joseph would be ready to handle it, and it would do him no harm. He was empowered to wait, and when you surrender to God's waiting period, you too will be *Empowered for Life.*

I believe that as you journey the roadway of an anointed, empowered lifestyle, you will be required by God to accept divine delays. The timing of God is so perfect and the restlessness of man is so consistently predictable. These two forces seem to wrestle with each other endlessly. When we accept the fact that God's desire for our lives is always the best, it makes it easier for us to accept our time in the waiting room, and understand that it does not represent a place of rejection, but a place of preparation for perfect positioning.

CHAPTER **10**

EMPOWERED FOR THE MOMENT

Then Pharaoh sent and called Joseph, and they brought him hastily out of the dungeon: and he shaved himself, and changed his raiment, and came in unto Pharaoh.   Genesis 41:14

Everything that Joseph had been through in previous years had been to prepare him for this moment. It is not an exaggeration to say that this was his moment of truth.

If Joseph had "blown it" anywhere along the way — with his brothers, with his father, in the pit, in captivity to the caravan drivers, in slavery in Potiphar's house, when he was falsely accused and unjustly imprisoned or when the butler failed to keep his commitment two years earlier to help him get out of prison — he might never have arrived at this moment. This was, without a doubt, the most important moment of his life, and he could not afford to mishandle his date with destiny. He was des-

tined to rule, and God knew how to bring that about, but what Joseph did in this moment could change everything.

I can see the king's men coming for Joseph and telling him that Pharaoh was calling for him. He quickly shaved and changed his clothes and went with them. It was as simple as that. Suddenly, the man who had attended to his character, the man who had attended to the deposit of the Spirit within him, the man who had kept his heart from bitterness, the man who had kept his spirit from wrath, the man who had walked in the ways of God, was about to have his day in the spotlight. Joseph was about to stand before Pharaoh.

How is it possible that a man of no former political experience, a man who had a prison record, a man who was little more than a slave, could stand before the great pharaoh of Egypt? It was because Joseph had determined early in life that his relationship with God was more valuable to him than anything else and because he had struggled at all costs to protect that relationship.

When Joseph had been hurt, he had to choose whether he would open his spirit to anger and bitterness or whether he would keep a sweet spirit before the Lord. When he was betrayed, he had to choose whether to give way to the temptation to seek vengeance or to put everything in God's hands and let Him deal with it. When people lied against him,

he had to choose whether he would lash back at them and demand that they restore his good name or whether he would pray for them and maintain his integrity before God. Everything was pointing toward this moment.

Joseph had been through all of that and more, yet he was so pure that even the heathen sought him out, recognizing that the Spirit of God was in him. He had made the right choices in life, had set the right priorities for his future, and it was paying off.

It might not have seemed so to others. Joseph's brothers certainly didn't embrace his dream and personal integrity and hated him because of them. Potiphar's wife certainly didn't agree with his holiness, and what he did infuriated her. Joseph had chosen, however, not to take the easy road, not to be guided by what others were thinking, and now the truth about his choices was about to be made known. He was summoned to the palace, and this was his moment of opportunity.

We all know how this came about. We heard it in Sunday school class when we were small children. When Pharaoh had his strange dreams, none of his advisors could imagine what they might mean. In all their discussion of dreams, someone remembered a man who was in prison who seemed to have a special gift in this regard. This was told to Pharaoh, and he called for Joseph immediately.

Fully two years had passed since Joseph had

interpreted the dream of the chief butler, but he was still anointed. He hadn't allowed his disappointment and the necessity of unjustly staying more years in prison keep him from maintaining a proper relationship with God. His gifts that had been manifested in the house of Potiphar and in his service in the prison were still active and powerful. They had, in fact, been developed even further.

Joseph had not known the exact moment his considerable talents would be called upon. He had no way of knowing, for sure, that Pharaoh would be his means of escape, although he had somehow sensed that it would be so. He had no way of knowing about Pharaoh's dream or that someone was being sought to interpret it. So when he was sent for, he was caught off guard in one sense, but the truth is that he had been preparing a lifetime for this moment. He had to shave and change his clothes before he was presentable enough to accompany the king's emissary. If he had known, he could have been ready. In reality, he was ready at all times.

And the fact is that Joseph was ready, spiritually speaking. A shave and a change of clothes was all that he needed to meet his appointment with destiny. This was Joseph's strength. He had kept his spirit pure through disappointment, temptation and the wrongs against him and had refused to allow his gifts to die.

He was ready. God had been with him in the pit.

He had been with him in Potiphar's house. He had been with him in the prison. And Joseph knew that God was with him now, as he hurriedly prepared to stand before Pharaoh.

Most of us men would have cut ourselves shaving that day or come out of the prison with mismatched socks on or something of that nature. Joseph had to be nervous as he prepared for this moment.

Or maybe not. Maybe the pit and the prison had prepared him for such a moment as this. He had had plenty of time alone over the past years to prepare. It was time now to make his mark on his generation, and he was strangely at peace. It was his time.

As Joseph was on his way to the palace, a thousand thoughts must have gone through his mind. What should he say? How should he say it? What would be required of him? What was the official protocol for appearing before a king?

Knowing the tempter as I do, I'm sure that he also whispered to Joseph, as the man of God was on his way to his moment of destiny:

"The last time you opened your mouth and used your prophetic gift, it resulted in a mess. You so upset your brothers that they sold you into slavery. If you open your mouth and tell Pharaoh what you think God is saying, you could make things worse, instead of better. You're in enough trouble

already. You don't want to do anything to complicate that further. You had better think long and hard about this whole holiness routine. Don't forget where it got you when you refused the offer of Potiphar's wife. Was that prison your great reward for righteousness?"

I'm convinced, however, that Joseph never considered remaining quiet that day in Pharaoh's presence. Compromise just wasn't part of his character.

When Joseph arrived at the palace, the king was full of praise:

> *And Pharaoh said unto Joseph, ... I have heard say of thee, that thou canst understand a dream to interpret it.* Genesis 41:15

Joseph's good fortune could have destroyed lesser men. Just think! The fame of him had reached the most powerful man in the world, and that man had called for his help. That's heady stuff! Joseph, however, was not about to be affected by flattery and insisted on setting the record straight up front. He wanted Pharaoh to know that he was not wise in himself and that his strength came from God:

> *And Joseph answered Pharaoh, saying, It is not in me: God shall give Pharaoh an answer of peace.* Genesis 41:16

124

Standing before the pharaoh must have been a terribly intimidating experience for Joseph. Most of us would have been intimidated, but Joseph knew that this was his moment. This was what God had told him about when he was a young boy. This was the prophetic significance of his father's having given him the coat of many colors. This was his destiny in God, so he was relaxed in the Spirit of the Lord.

With all this in mind, Joseph might have been forgiven if he had started some political negotiation with Pharaoh or if he had entered into some philosophical or intellectual rationalization. But he didn't. The power of God had gotten him this far, and it would get him the rest of the way. He had operated in the authority and favor of his anointing to this point, and that anointing would be sufficient for the rest of his journey. He would interpret Pharaoh's dreams by the Spirit, and no other way.

Those dreams are just as interesting to us now as they were when we were children: seven fat cows followed by seven skinny cows, and seven good ears followed by seven poor ones. What could this mean?

As he listened to the king tell the dreams, Joseph refused to panic. This was a man in need, and he was sure that God would give him an answer for the king, just as He had revealed the meaning of

dreams to him many times before. He was not wondering what he could ask for if he did get the interpretation right and was offered a reward. Some of us would have been quickly repenting of wrong attitudes or begging for time to fast and pray to get our spirits right so that we could hear from God. Joseph did not have to do any of these things. It was time for him to seize the moment of God-given opportunity, and he was ready.

The fact that Pharaoh was expecting an answer to his questions and that kings had often been known to fly into a rage when someone did not know what to answer to their inquiries did not seem to bother Joseph. He was ready. He didn't require additional time to think or pray about it. He was anointed, and his gift was in operation — as it had been at other times and in other places.

Joseph was not having a bad day. He was not on a vacation from spiritual things. He was ready, as always, and quickly gave the interpretation of the dreams. They revealed that there would be seven years of plenty in the region, and in those years crops would do unusually well. This period of plenty would be followed by seven very lean years, and in those years crops would fail in many sectors.

This was not just a lucky guess based on the weather patterns Joseph had observed on his way to the palace. This was the perfect, God-sent interpretation of the dreams, a direct result of Joseph's

anointed lifestyle. He did not have to work up an answer or pray one down. This anointing for knowing mysteries was part of his everyday life. He was a man of dreams and interpretations.

This time, however, Joseph went further. He didn't stop with the interpretation of the dreams themselves, but went on to tell Pharaoh what he must do in response to the dreams in order to avoid tragedy. The dreams were for a reason, and Joseph went on to address that reason:

> *And Joseph said unto Pharaoh, ... God hath showed Pharaoh what he is about to do.*
>
> Genesis 41:25

God had not only showed Joseph that famine was coming; He also showed him how to get ready for the famine. And when the famine eventually came, seven years later, Egypt was ready for it and could prosper more in the time of want than it had in the time of plenty. Joseph's administrative gift was now being manifested.

Joseph told Pharaoh that he should appoint a wise man to head the collection, storage and distribution of food, and his instructions became even more detailed. Special officers should be appointed throughout the land, and a fifth of the available farmland should be used to produce grain during

the good years. This grain should be stored in various cities for use during the bad times.

Giving advice to a king is nothing to play with, and those who do it had better know that their advice is sound. If not, they are liable to lose their heads. This was not child's play. It was a dangerous business.

But Joseph was not stabbing in the dark. This was not a hit-or-miss proposition. He had walked with God in the good times and the bad, and because he had refused to allow anything to hinder his relationship with God, his prophetic gift was in operation, and his message was right on target.

Now it could be seen that Joseph was more than a dreamer. He was more than a visionary. He was more than a man with a gift. He was a man of destiny who had learned to walk in such a way that he was respected and trusted, and great authority was, therefore, given to him.

When Joseph's moment of truth had come, the pharaoh listened attentively as the foreign prisoner offered his God-inspired advice. Then, as we are about to see, Pharaoh not only heeded that advice; he put Joseph in charge of the entire operation.

How was that possible? Because this young man was empowered for the moment in order to be *Empowered for Life.*

I believe there are God-given, strategic, season-changing moments that come to us as we live anointed, empowered lifestyles. We must be ready to seize these moments of life-changing destiny. It happens in business, when the deal of a lifetime is thrust upon you. It happens in career, when you're being interviewed for a promotion that will ultimately change your future. It happens in relationships: "Is he [or she] the one that I'm to spend the rest of my life with?" It happens in church, when eternal souls are on the line.

Being empowered to seize the moment doesn't happen in that particular moment. The empowerment of the moment is the culmination of a surrendered life that has been yielded to an all-knowing God.

CHAPTER 11

EMPOWERED TO RULE

And the thing was good in the eyes of Pharaoh, and in the eyes of all his servants. And Pharaoh said unto his servants, Can we find such a one as this is, a man in whom the Spirit of God is?

Genesis 41:37-38

Pharaoh liked what he was hearing, and he liked what he was seeing in Joseph. People who are both wise and modest are hard to find, and Pharaoh was sure he had just found one such person. Most people he knew would have tried to wrest from him some concession, some personal favor, before answering him anything at all. He had seen it too many times and knew what most people wanted even before they spoke. What they said had to be examined to see what motivation was behind it.

Joseph seemed to be the exception. He had asked nothing for himself and seemed genuinely interested in the welfare of the Egyptian people. His answer

not only made sense, but something about both the man and what he was saying seemed to ring true. Joseph was totally transparent and honest, refreshingly different from the average "royal counselor" the king was accustomed to dealing with. He was impressed.

This is truly amazing! It's not easy to impress a king. Such men have seen a little of everything and often surround themselves with the wisest of men from many nations. There was something visibly different about Joseph, and it touched a chord in Pharaoh's heart.

Even though he was a pagan man, Pharaoh somehow realized that what Joseph had said was *"good,"* and his servants felt the same way. This was a great miracle, and it came about because of the anointing of God upon Joseph's life. We cannot get anything *"good"* accomplished in life unless we are anointed. The Bible shows that even the *"good"* done by Jesus came about because of His anointing:

> *How God anointed Jesus of Nazareth with the Holy Ghost and with power: who went about doing good, and healing all that were oppressed of the devil; for God was with him.*   Acts 10:38

When Joseph moved in the anointing, the outcome was *"good"* in the eyes of the pharaoh. God can give us favor with those who are, for all intents

and purposes, diametrically opposed to who we are and what we do. The anointing removes every barrier and causes us to be at peace with our enemies. God has even promised to make our enemies our "footstool."

Pharaoh was moved in a strange way by Joseph's anointing, moved to actions that he would surely question in the future. He believed this man Joseph. He wasn't sure why, but he felt that Joseph was right about bad times coming. None of his counselors could have foreseen it, and nobody would like to accept it, but somehow he knew it was true.

And if bad times were coming, who better to have at his side than a man of confidence like Joseph? He quickly looked around him, to see the reaction of his counselors, and he could see in their faces the same awe and respect he felt for this young man with the prophetic gift. So, without any further private consultation with his aides and advisors, Pharaoh suddenly made Joseph a proposal:

And Pharaoh said unto Joseph, Forasmuch as God hath showed thee all this, there is none so discreet and wise as thou art : thou shalt be over my house, and according unto thy word shall all my people be ruled: only in the throne will I be greater than thou. And Pharaoh said unto Joseph, See, I have set thee over all the land of Egypt.

Genesis 41:39-41

This is getting more amazing by the moment! Joseph had been brought directly from the jail to the palace, and yet a learned and experienced ruler such as Pharaoh was now making a prisoner head over all that he had, without asking anyone else what he thought about it. What a miracle!

Joseph would not only be over Pharaoh's *"house,"* meaning his kingdom, but he would also be over all of Pharaoh's staff as well. He was being given a position higher than any of Pharaoh's other staff members. Only Pharaoh himself would be more powerful, and only in the sense that he held the throne. All other authority was to be placed in Joseph's hands. What an amazing decision!

To seal this rash decision, Pharaoh made a further move:

> *And Pharaoh took off his ring from his hand, and put it upon Joseph's hand, and arrayed him in vestures of fine linen, and put a gold chain about his neck; and he made him to ride in the second chariot which he had; and they cried before him, Bow the knee: and he made him ruler over all the land of Egypt.* Genesis 41:42-43

The same Joseph who had been despised by his brothers and rebuked by his father, the same man who had been sold into slavery, the same man who

had been slandered by his owner's wife and unjustly imprisoned was now *"ruler over all the land of Egypt."* That's what the anointing will do for you. No one could keep Joseph down because he had God-given authority. Pharaoh was just confirming what God had already done for Joseph. Joseph's authority did not come from Pharaoh; it came from God Himself. An anointed lifestyle will bring forth the manifestation of God's favor.

This miracle that God gave Joseph went far beyond just getting out of jail. It was more than recovering his dignity and respect. It went further than material possessions. Joseph had moved beyond rejection and rebuke, beyond slander and abuse, and was moving into favor, so much so that no one could lift a finger in Egypt without first getting permission from him. That's what God does for those who give Him free reign in their lives.

Pharaoh must have wondered in the days and weeks to come what had possessed him to do such a rash thing. In a moment's time, he had put all the power of his realm into the hands of a man he didn't even know well — and a felon at that. Pharaoh had not called for Potiphar to testify about what he knew of Joseph. He had not called in any prison officials to review Joseph's record. He had been impressed with Joseph, and nothing else mattered at the moment. He was satisfied with his decision.

The closest aides and the various members of

Pharaoh's family must have complained about this rash act in the days to come. It *was* strange and *would* make anyone wonder. Pharaoh had mysteriously come under the spell of the anointing, and he probably found it difficult to explain to others and, perhaps, even to himself.

Still, he didn't change his mind in the days immediately following. He didn't rescind his order. He didn't fire Joseph or send him back to prison, and he didn't replace him or weaken his authority. Everything about Joseph seemed *"good"* in the eyes of Pharaoh and in the eyes of all his servants, and Egypt prospered under the command of its new prime minister.

Just as God had blessed the house of Potiphar because of Joseph, and just as God had blessed Joseph's work in the prison, now all of Egypt would reap the benefit of his anointing. Whatever he touched would prosper — because God was with him.

When Pharaoh first noted the *"good"* in Joseph, he said something very strange to his servants: *"Can we find such a one as this is, a man in whom the Spirit of God is?"* This word Spirit is not with a small "s," so it means that the pharaoh was recognizing God's Spirit in Joseph's life. This word God is also not with a small "g," so Pharaoh was recognizing Jehovah Himself as the Source of Joseph's wisdom. Pharaoh

was a wise man himself in that he immediately attributed Joseph's power to divinity.

Pharaoh was surely a pagan, a heathen, an idol-worshiping man, and yet he was saying that he knew he could find no better man for the job, because the living God was in this young man. That's powerful! And I'm convinced that God wants to do this same miracle for more of us in the days in which we are now living.

Suddenly Joseph had a royal ring on his finger. Suddenly he was dressed in fine linen. Suddenly he had a gold chain around his neck. Suddenly he had a custom-built chariot. Suddenly he had men running before him shouting, "Bow the knee!" Suddenly everything that God had said to him many years before, when he was still a very young boy, now made sense. Suddenly his dreams were no longer silly, as they had seemed to others at the time they were first told. What had come to Joseph was a revelation from God, and because he clung to that revelation and refused to let go of it, God was bringing it all to pass.

God was not at all surprised by this turn of events. He knew exactly who Joseph was to become, and His intention for each of us can be more powerful than every circumstance that tries to speak against us as we move toward the fulfillment of our calling in Him.

Joseph had just come from the prison, and the

only thing about him that was different from the man who had been unjustly imprisoned for so many years was that he had taken a bath and shaved and put on different clothes. That might have changed his physical appearance dramatically, but it could not change what he was on the inside. I'm afraid that many of us require far more than a shave and a change of clothes. Joseph had learned to walk with God, and now God's touch was visible upon his life.

Joseph had power with God. The seeds of it had been in him since childhood, and he had nurtured them and caused them to grow with each new experience and with each new challenge in life. He had refused to let these seeds die, despite the fact that others had consistently wronged him. His power had been there when he was thrown into the pit, it had been there when he was sold to the Ismaelites, it had been there when he was serving Potiphar, it had been there when he was thrown unjustly into prison, and it was still there. It had not grown weak with time. His gift was now at peak performance, and he was ready to serve the pharaoh.

Joseph would no longer have to carry a key chain around, as he had in Potiphar's house and in the prison. The guards over the treasure houses of Egypt would now recognize his authority and open to him when he required it. He could go in and out as he wished, do an audit of the goods in stock, require an answer of any servant or do anything else he

wanted. He had full authority. It had been given to him by the king himself. From that day forward, none dared disobey Joseph's command, for it was backed by Pharaoh himself.

Joseph had endured a difficult journey to get to this place. It is hard to imagine being so severely betrayed by your own brothers that they would sell you into slavery. That was no boyish prank. It was malicious, and it would have affected most of us very deeply. Some people never recover from treatment much less severe.

In Potiphar's house, Joseph had done more than an excellent job. He made sure that everything pertaining to his master was well managed, and the thanks he had received was to be thrown into prison. About that time, many of the believers I know would have been ready to give up on God. These days, in fact, people seem to turn their backs on God for the flimsiest reasons, usually because they don't get what they want or they don't get it when they want it.

Joseph, however, had endured every trial along the way, and now he was presented with a new day, a new and wonderful opportunity. If he had been able to accomplish something in the past, now he could accomplish much more. There would be no comparison between his past accomplishments and what he was about to do. This was his day, the reason for which he had been born.

Now, within moments, Pharaoh had made Joseph

second in charge in his empire (Prime Minister of Egypt in today's terms) and had placed in his hands all authority. From that moment on, he said, no one would make a move in Egypt without first consulting Joseph. Nothing would be done without his permission. And no one could overrule him except the pharaoh himself.

I wonder how Potiphar felt when he saw Joseph riding by his house in that gleaming chariot. I wonder what he thought when he saw everyone bowing to this Hebrew. When God destines a thing for us, nobody alive can stop it. Those who try to curse us will, themselves, be cursed, and every curse offered against us will turn into a blessing for us.

When it all happens, we must admit, "There's no way this could have happened in the natural," and we must give God all the glory. There is no way that Joseph could have planned things and positioned himself to meet and impress the pharaoh. He would never have dreamed of being put in prison as a means of bringing all this to pass. Who would have imagined that the pharaoh would have respect for an inmate, and a hated Hebrew at that? It didn't make sense.

Parolees have a hard time finding decent jobs. They have a hard time building up respect within the community where they settle. They have a hard time developing a normal home life. Parolees have a lot of strikes against them, and they don't normally

become prime ministers, especially not overnight, as in Joseph's case. This was a miracle from God.

God somehow let Pharaoh know that he would never find another man as wise as Joseph. Could the king have judged that in just a few moments of interview with Joseph? I think not. What a miracle!

As I said, Pharaoh probably later wondered at his own rash actions. Probably, when he was second-guessed by other advisors, he would think back over everything he had done that day and wonder what had possessed him. Yet, at the time, he knew he was doing the right thing. He instantly recognized the Spirit of God in this matter and instantly knew that this man was wise.

So, before he knew what was happening, he had taken off one of his golden rings and put it on Joseph's finger, he had taken off a gold chain and hung it around Joseph's neck, and his gold-plated Mercedes chariot was pulling up to the curb to pick up Joseph and whisk him off to a victory parade through the city.

As Joseph soon found himself riding around the city, I can imagine him saying, "I am empowered to rule in order to be *Empowered for Life.*"

I believe that in living an anointed, empowered lifestyle, we ultimately come to a place that everything that God has allowed us to learn, to endure and to develop comes to its predestined moment of fruition. Walking in authority is the result of yielding to the will of God in multiple areas. Good rulers have character. Good rulers always have a dream. Good rulers never lose their servant hearts. Good rulers endure, serve and wait, all the while respecting the benefits of the life of holiness. Good rulers, therefore, inherit, prosper and are favored. You may rule over a church, a business or a family, but whereever you rule, I pray that you rule well.

CHAPTER 12

EMPOWERED FOR LIFE

And the LORD was with Joseph, and he was a prosperous man; and he was in the house of his master the Egyptian. And his master saw that the LORD was with him, and that the LORD made all that he did to prosper in his hand. Genesis 39:2-3

When I set about to write this book, my desire was not to simply present another narrative of the life of Joseph. I considered him to be the ultimate prototype of the anointed, empowered lifestyle.

Too often the spiritual people among us seem to have lost the practical skills they need to be successful in life, and the practical people among us seem not to possess the spiritual virtues that would bring them ultimate success. Joseph had it all: incredible brilliance, impeccable character and uncompromised holiness. He was the type of man that we should all aspire to be. He was truly anointed.

Joseph prophesied with profound accuracy and authority. He administrated with a brilliance that would have made him a multi-billionaire in today's economic climate. But he was also a man of virtues: his commitment to his father, his endurance of hardship, his servant heart and his forgiving nature were all commendable.

But Joseph was not the seed of the Holy Ghost; he was a man born of corruptible seed, just like we have been. He was different because he learned to yield to the hand of God and lived to benefit from his surrender.

Few have ever prophesied as Joseph prophesied. Few have ever been supernaturally promoted and favored as he was. Few have ever seized the moment like he seized it. He truly was the image of what an anointed man should be.

And what about us? Should we have great gifts in the Holy Spirit and yet struggle each day to organize the affairs of our lives? Should we have great spiritual experiences, but not enough common sense to balance our check books, invest wisely and prepare a secure future for our children and grandchildren?

I don't believe God allowed Joseph to be one of the most prolific characters in the Bible for us to look at him like a fictitious superhero. He, I believe, was the original anointed man who was birthed out of the common ground we all share called imperfec-

144

tion. I pray that we can learn, through prayer and surrender, to allow the Holy Spirit to link together in our lives the key elements that we see exemplified in Joseph that caused his God-ordained rise to greatness.

The spiritual man must pray for the practical empowerments that so graced Joseph. Those of you who are more cerebral and unemotionally practical in your approach to life need to pray for the impassioned spirituality that possessed Joseph all of his life. Life is not just to be lived; life should be anointed and empowered, because an abundant life is vastly superior to a frustrated existence.

My prayer for you is that the virtues of God we see manifested in Joseph be loosed in you, that you may truly be *Empowered for Life.*

POSSESSING your PROPHETIC PROMISE

Tim Bagwell

Possessing Your Prophetic Promise

At a time when the Church has been blessed by the greatest period of expository teaching in the Word of God that any generation has ever experienced, at a time when we have more resources available to us than ever before, why do so many of God's people seem to wander for years in the wilderness without ever experiencing a breakthrough into the fullness of what God has promised to them? Why have so many received miraculous provision and protection but still have not scratched the surface of their spiritual potential? It is time to possess our prophetic promises.

But what must we do to cross over the river Jordan and possess our Promised Land? What steps are necessary to dislodge every enemy and take back what is rightfully ours? In this book, Dr. Tim Bagwell brings forth, as only he can, the revelation that God has given to him to bring YOU to the place of *Possessing Your Prophetic Promise*.

ISBN 1-884369-12-X $9.99

DR. TIM BAGWELL

Foreword by Oral Roberts

When I
See
The
Blood

When I See the Blood

- Why is it that most modern-day Christians have chosen to virtually ignore the message of the blood of Christ?

- Why is it that this all-important theme is not being preached more, sung more and taught more these days?

- Could it be that the enemy of our souls is trying to silence a message that is most important to the welfare of our souls and our continuing victory as Christians?

With convincing authority, Tim Bagwell declares that the age-old message of the blood is still valid for our time and that many of the false doctrines that have invaded the church today have come about because we lack revelation regarding this foundational truth.

ISBN 1-884369-74-X $9.99

EMPOWERED
for the
CALL

Understanding the Dynamics of the Anointing

Dr. Tim Bagwell

Empowered for the Call

"An end-time prophet, pastor and teacher, Tim Bagwell literally exemplifies the empowerment of the call of God on a believer's life. *Empowered for the Call* plumbs the depth and breadth of God's anointing power. It is a valuable addition to every Christian's library."
— Oral Roberts, Oral Roberts University

"In this generation, the Lord has raised up strategic leaders equipped by the experience of time and testing and with a godly compassion to empower the Church to face the challenges of this fast-paced information age in which we live. Tim Bagwell is one of those rare individuals whose gifted spirit, transparent character and integrity is a welcome breath of fresh air. I highly recommend his relevant and timely message to all those who desire truth. It lays down principles that are destined to impact your life and the world around you."
— Dr. Myles Munroe, Bahamas Faith Ministries

"Tim Bagwell, a twentieth-century prophet, dares to put into manuscript form God's challenging concepts on the anointing."
— Dr. Ralph Wilkerson, Melodyland Christian Center

"Tim Bagwell is once again on the cutting edge with this much-needed book. It's in-depth, yet fast-paced. Tim Bagwell has captured the essence of all that is inherent in the anointing power of God."
— Evangelist Tim Storey, Tim Storey Ministries

ISBN 1-884369-73-1 $9.99

Ministry address:

Dr. Tim Bagwell
8700 E Park Meadows Drive
Lone Tree, Colorado 80124